How to Pass

English for Business

First Level

How to Pass English for Business First Level

1. Auflage 1994
2. Auflage 1997

© **Copyright Logophon Lehrmittel Verlag GmbH**

All rights reserved. No part of this publication may be reproduced, stored in a retrieval system, or transmitted in any form or by any means, electronic, photocopying, recording or otherwise, without prior permission of the publisher.

Das Werk ist in allen seinen Teilen urheberrechtlich geschützt. Jede Verwendung ist ohne Zustimmung des Verlages unzulässig. Das gilt ins besondere für Vervielfältigungen, Übersetzungen, Mikroverfilmung und die Einspeicherung in und Verarbeitung durch elektronische Systeme.

ISBN 3-922514-30-8

Published by: Logophon Lehrmittel Verlag
Alte Gärtnerei 2
55128 Mainz, Germany

Layout: Lynne M Evans

Printed and bound in Slovakia.

Other books in this series:

How to Pass English for Business Second Level
ISBN 3-922514-31-6

How to Pass English for Business Third Level
ISBN 3-922514-32-4

ACKNOWLEDGEMENTS

The authors would like to thank all those who have helped in writing this book.

Many thanks also to John and Lucy Davison, Astrid Feistel, Anna Silanova, Lynne Evans, Ivan Midgley and Petra Wächter.

Special thanks to Martin Billingham and Rupert Jones Parry at the LCCIEB.

Special thanks to the LCCIEB, to Jean-Pierre Jouteux, Pierre Semidei and Gabriele Schaub at Logophon.

FOREWORD

Peter Godwin CBE

I am delighted to commend this book to assist students in attaining success in English for Business.

With English recognised as the world's transactional language, an ability to use it fluently represents a considerable advantage and the London Chamber of Commerce and Industry certificate has become recognised as an international passport to employment.

The LCCI Examinations Board was set up over a hundred years ago to provide qualifications created **by** the business community **for** the business community. It is now at the forefront of vocational education and development, operating in more than 80 countries throughout the world.

English for Business focuses heavily on practical and realistic communicative tasks in a work environment. Support materials will prove vital to both teachers and candidates worldwide in achieving good results. I believe that this new series of textbooks on "How to Pass English for Business" will provide excellent, clear, systematic guidelines to help candidates achieve their aims and, in this increasingly qualification-led world, an LCCIEB certificate in English for Business can give an undoubted edge to those wishing to operate in international business circles.

Peter Godwin CBE
Managing Director, West Merchant Bank Limited
Chairman, Asia Pacific Advisory Group

FOREWORD

This book has been written for students preparing for the First Level of English for Business. It is designed for use in class and as self-study.

By looking in detail at past papers it provides a thorough break-down of the types of questions that have occurred over the last few years, together with an effective way of dealing with them. The student is guided stage by stage through the questions, receiving advice on what to include and, just as importantly, what to exclude.

Each question is accompanied by model answers, and there is no doubt that a student who follows this step by step approach and emulates the language used in the answers will score highly on similar questions in the examination itself.

Martin Billingham
Chief Examiner
English for Business First Level

Contents

Introduction I

Specimen Certificate III

Section 1:   Letters 1

Section 2:   Memos 25

Section 3:   Short Answers 47

Section 4:   True or False 77

Section 5:   Gap-Fills 105

Section 6:   Forms and Diagrams 129

Answer Key 153

Specimen Paper 187

INTRODUCTION

This book is for candidates preparing for the First Level of the London Chamber of Commerce and Industry Examinations Board English for Business Examination.

It can be used either as a class book or for self-study. It contains 6 sections which look at those tasks which are likely to come up in the examination, namely:

- Letters
- Memos
- Short Answers
- True or False
- Gap-Fills
- Forms and Diagrams

At the back of the book there is an **Answer Key**. Each section has an Introduction which explains to the student how to approach the question.

The sections on Letters and Memos are divided up and take the student through the following 6 stages:

- Identify the Task
- Layout
- Identify Relevant Information
- Group/Order Relevant Information
- Write the Answer
- Check the Answer

Practice 1 provides the student with an example of how to complete the task. In each subsequent practice the student has to complete one more stage. By Practice 7 the student completes all the stages alone.

Three questions are then provided as further practice and suggested answers to all the practice questions can be found at the back of the book.

	STAGES					
	1	2	3	4	5	6
Practice 1	○	○	○	○	○	○
Practice 2	○	○	○	○	○	☐
Practice 3	○	○	○	○	☐	☐
Practice 4	○	○	○	☐	☐	☐
Practice 5	○	○	☐	☐	☐	☐
Practice 6	○	☐	☐	☐	☐	☐
Practice 7	☐	☐	☐	☐	☐	☐
Practice 8	☐	☐	☐	☐	☐	☐
Practice 9	☐	☐	☐	☐	☐	☐
Practice 10	☐	☐	☐	☐	☐	☐

○ Stages already completed.   Student completes stage ☐

The sections on Short Answers, True or False, Gap-Fills and Forms and Diagrams are divided up and take the student through the following 4 stages:

- Identify the Task
- What to do Before you Start
- Write the Answer
- Check the Answer

INTRODUCTION

Practice 1 provides the student with an example of how to complete the task. In each subsequent practice the student has to complete one more stage. By Practice 5 the student completes all the stages alone.

Five questions are then provided as further practice and suggested answers to all the practice questions can be found at the back of the book.

	STAGES			
	1	2	3	4
Practice 1	○	○	○	○
Practice 2	○	○	○	□
Practice 3	○	○	□	□
Practice 4	○	□	□	□
Practice 5	□	□	□	□
Practice 6	□	□	□	□
Practice 7	□	□	□	□
Practice 8	□	□	□	□
Practice 9	□	□	□	□
Practice 10	□	□	□	□

○ Stages already completed.　　　　　　　　　　Student completes stage □

The Examination

The examination consists of 4 questions, all of which are to be answered. These questions are described by the LCCIEB as:

a   "The composition of a letter, or memo communicating with an organisation or between organisations.

b   A prose passage of about 300 words for comprehension. The brief answers required will oblige candidates to relate and use information **across the passage**, not merely to reproduce it in sequence.

c   A "look and think" comprehension task, based on some graphic or numerical display stimulus and requiring only short answers.

d   A "look and write" production task, where candidates will have to label a diagram, flow chart or organisation tree, fill in a form or questionnaire, or re-order and supplement data."

The examination lasts for 2 hours and it is important for students to practise answering questions and whole papers within the time allowed.

"Candidates" according to the LCCIEB, "will receive credit for good grammar, accuracy, style, layout and maturity of expression. "Incorrect spelling and punctuation will be penalised.

For further information regarding the organisation and administration of the English for Business Examinations, contact:

　　　　　　　London Chamber of Commerce and Industry Examinations Board
　　　　　　　Marlowe House
　　　　　　　Station Road
　　　　　　　Sidcup
　　　　　　　Kent
　　　　　　　DA15 7BJ
　　　　　　　England

　　　　　　　Tel　　　0181 302 0261
　　　　　　　Fax　　　0181 309 5169

10000000

LONDON CHAMBER
of
COMMERCE AND INDUSTRY
EXAMINATIONS BOARD

Certificate

This is to certify that

A N OTHER

has been examined by the Examinations Board of the London Chamber of Commerce and Industry and has been found qualified to receive this Certificate for proficiency as shown below.

First Level Single Subjects

English for Business   Pass****
****

Examinations Series   FOUR 1993   Centre   YTEST /0001

Sir James Duncan
Chairman, Commercial Education Trust

W. J. Swords
Chief Executive of the Examinations Board

Simon Sperryn
Chief Executive of the Chamber

SECTION 1: Letters

Introduction

Question 1 is always either a letter or a memo. This section looks at letters.

Stage 1: Identify the Task

There is usually a situation given and then a task set. Read the "situation" through until you know who you are, who you work for and what the situation is. When you know this, read through the "task" at least once until you know who you're writing to and exactly what you are asked to do. The instructions normally read "Lay your answer out as a letter".

Stage 2: Layout

Normal layout is:

your company address:	top right hand corner
date:	top right hand corner below sender's address
name/address of recipient:	beneath date on left hand side
correct salutation:	"Dear..."
complimentary close:	Yours sincerely (Dear (Name)) Yours faithfully (Dear Sir/Madam/Sirs)
signature:	your signature
name:	printed name
position:	your position

Example of layout

> 24 High Street
> Newcastle
> NE46 4AB
>
> 29th March 1993
>
> Mr J Smith *(inside address)*
> 28 Broom Street
> Hexham
> NE71 2SV
>
> Dear Mr Smith
>
> ....
> ....
>
> Yours sincerely
>
> *Ena Brown*
>
> Ena Brown
> Sales Manager

Stage 3: Identify Relevant Information

Decide exactly why you are writing, what information you need to give or what information you need to receive. You are often asked to make up any necessary information. This may include your position, name of company and address, as well as other details.

Stage 4: Group/Order Relevant Information

Group the information in the best way and then order it so that one point follows on to the next.

Stage 5: Write the Letter

Language in letters is usually polite. Useful starting phrases are "Thank you for your letter of 2nd January 1989", or "I am writing to you because..." A useful finishing phrase is "I look forward to hearing from you."

Stage 6: Check your Work

Checklist: Letter

The following is a list of points to check when you write a letter.

1 Have you completed the task?

2 Is your layout correct?

3 Do you have all the correct information?

4 Is it ordered in the best way?

5 Is the language appropriate for a letter?

6 Have you checked spelling, grammar and punctuation?

SECTION 1

Practice 1

Situation: You are the Marketing Manager of a computer company, and a local college has written to your department asking if you would consider sponsoring their week-long drama festival to be held in the summer.

Task: Write a letter to the Principal of the college explaining that while you sympathise with their aims and needs, your company has a fixed budget for sponsorship and no new ventures can be considered until next year.

Note: *Layout your answer as a letter. Make up any necessary details.*
(Series 3, 1991, Q1)

Stage 1: Identify the Task

Lay out your answer as a letter.

Stage 2: Layout

- your company address - Funtime Computers Ltd, 28 Blackwell Street, Newcastle, NE12 4AB
- the date - 28th June 1991
- the name and address of the person to whom you are writing - The Principal, Newcastle College of Technology, 35 High Street, Newcastle, NE14 3LJ
- the correct salutation - Dear Sir/Madam
- complimentary close - Yours faithfully
- a signature - your signature
- name - your printed name
- position - Marketing Manager

Stage 3: Identify Relevant Information

- interested to hear about drama festival
- sympathise with aims
- unable to help
- fixed budget for sponsorship
- no new ventures until next year
- good luck with sponsorship
- hope all goes well
- try again next year

Stage 4: Group/Order Relevant Information

1. Thanks for letter.
2. Interested to hear about drama festival.
3. Sympathise with aims and needs.
4. Unfortunately unable to help.
5. Fixed budget for sponsorship.
6. No new ventures until next year.
7. Hope it all goes well.
8. Perhaps try again next year.
9. Good luck.

Stage 5: Write the Letter

                                                                     Funtime Computers Ltd
                                                                     28 Blackwell Street
                                                                     Newcastle
                                                                     NE12 4AB

                                                                     28th June 1991

The Principal
Newcastle College of Technology
35 High Street
Newcastle
NE14 3LJ

Dear Sir/Madam

Thank you for your letter of 24th June.

I was very interested to hear about the drama festival you are holding in the summer and sympathise with your aims and needs.

Unfortunately I am unable to help you as our company has a fixed budget for sponsorship and at present no new ventures will be considered until next year.

I hope your festival is successful and can only suggest that perhaps you contact us again next year.

In the meantime, good luck!

Yours faithfully

(your signature)
(printed name)
Marketing Manager

Stage 6: Check your Work ☑

Checklist: Letter

1. Have you completed the task? ☑
2. Is your layout correct? ☑
3. Do you have all the correct information? ☑
4. Is it ordered in the best way? ☑
5. Is the language appropriate for a letter? ☑
6. Have you checked spelling, grammar and punctuation? ☑

SECTION 1

Practice 2

Situation: A company which manufactures balloons carrying advertising slogans has asked you to organise a display of its products for one week in the foyer of a local hotel.

Task: From the offices of your marketing consultancy, write a letter to the manager of a local hotel, explaining that you would like to rent space in his hotel. Specify the sort of display stand you would like to erect and other necessary details. Make up the name and address of your company and any other necessary information.

(Series 4, 1992, Q1)

Stage 1: Identify the Task

Write a letter.

Stage 2: Layout

- your company address - Expert Marketing Consultants, 21 Blackett Street, Manchester, MC1 3PQ
- the date - 1st November 1992
- the name and address of the person to whom you are writing - The Manager, Hotel Grande, 13 Fore Street, Manchester, MC3 7NJ
- the correct salutation - Dear Sir/Madam
- complimentary close - Yours faithfully
- a signature - your signature
- name - your printed name
- position - Marketing Manager

Stage 3: Identify Relevant Information

- display of products of balloon company
- want to rent space in the hotel
- one week
- display stand should be platform
- in a corner of foyer
- tables
- size of stand should be 4m x 8m
- balloons carry advertising slogans
- should be of interest to hotel business customers
- make an appointment to discuss further details

Stage 4: Group/Order Relevant Information

1. Want to rent space in hotel foyer.
2. For a display of products of a balloon company.
3. Balloons carry advertising slogans.
4. Should be of interest to hotel business customers.
5. Display stand would be a platform, with samples of products and tables and chairs.
6. Size of stand should be 4m x 8 m.
7. Last for a week.
8. Ideally would be in a corner.
9. Make an appointment to discuss details.
10. Hope to hear from you.

Letters

Stage 5: Write the Letter

Expert Marketing Consultants
21 Blackett Street
Manchester
MC1 3PQ

1st November 1992

The Manager
Hotel Grande
13 Fore Street
Manchester
MC3 7NJ

Dear Sir/Madam

I am writing to you on behalf of a customer of ours who would like to rent some space in your hotel foyer in order to display their products.

The company produce balloons which carry advertising slogans, therefore the display would probably be interesting for your business customers.

The display stand would be a platform with chairs and tables, and contain samples of the company's products. The stand would be 4m x 8m and the display would last for a week. For best effect the stand should be located in a light corner of the foyer.

If you are interested I suggest we meet personally to discuss details.

I look forward to hearing from you.

Yours faithfully

(your signature)
(printed name)
Marketing Manager

Now complete the following stage.

Stage 6: Check your Work ☑

Checklist: Letter

1. Have you completed the task? ☐
2. Is your layout correct? ☐
3. Do you have all the correct information? ☐
4. Is it ordered in the best way? ☐
5. Is the language appropriate for a letter? ☐
6. Have you checked spelling, grammar and punctuation? ☐

SECTION 1

Practice 3

Situation: You are working temporarily in your local tourist office and your boss has asked you to find a writer to produce a short guide to your town/city.

Task: A colleague, Archie Leach, has recommended a friend of his, Michael Rees, the famous author of the "London Book". Write to Mr Rees, at 21 Meadowcourt Road, London, SE3 9EU, asking if he would be interested in the project. Specify what you want and the details of payment.

Note: Lay your answer out as a **letter** and make up any necessary details.
(Series 2, 1993, Q1)

Stage 1: Identify the Task

Lay your answer out as a letter.

Stage 2: Layout

- your company address - Tourist Office, 19 Eldon Gardens, Perth, PH13 4NL
- the date - 28th April 1993
- the name and address of the person to whom you are writing - Mr M Rees, 21 Meadowcourt Road, London, SE3 9EU
- the correct salutation - Dear Mr Rees
- complimentary close - Yours sincerely
- a signature - your signature
- name - your printed name
- position - no position

Stage 3: Identify Relevant Information

- want a writer to produce guide
- Archie Leach gave his name
- already written "The London Guide"
- is he interested in the project?
- guide would include:
  - places to visit
  - places to eat
  - places of historical interest
  - places of outstanding beauty
- payment
  - expenses during research period
  - sum in advance
  - percentage of every book sold

Stage 4: Group/Order Relevant Information

1. Need someone to write a short guide.
2. Got his name through Archie Leach, a colleague.
3. Know of his book "The London Book".
4. Required guide would give information on:
   - places to visit
   - places of historical interest
   - places of outstanding beauty
   - places to eat
5. Payment would be:
   - a sum in advance
   - expenses during research
   - percentage of every book sold
6. If he's interested, meet to discuss details.

Now complete the following stages.

Stage 5: Write the Letter

Stage 6: Check your Work ☑

Checklist: Letter

1. Have you completed the task? ☐
2. Is your layout correct? ☐
3. Do you have all the correct information? ☐
4. Is it ordered in the best way? ☐
5. Is the language appropriate for a letter? ☐
6. Have you checked spelling, grammar and punctuation? ☐

SECTION 1

Practice 4

Situation: The firm for which your work, European Management Consultancy, has just developed a Special Intensive Course for Managers.

Task: You work in the Marketing Department of this consultancy firm and send a brochure containing details of this course to the Personnel Manager of a local company. Write a **short covering letter** to accompany this brochure, mentioning briefly the reasons for developing the course, its contents, the date, the place and the cost.

Note: *Lay out your answer as a **letter**. Make up any necessary details.*

(Series 3, 1992, Q1)

Stage 1: Identify the Task
Write a short covering letter.

Stage 2: Layout

- your company address - European Management Consultancy, 21 High Street, London, W1
- the date - 26th June 1992
- the name and address of the person to whom you are writing - The Personnel Manager, Funtime Computers, 19 Market Street, London, W1
- the correct salutation - Dear Sir/Madam
- complimentary close - Yours faithfully
- a signature - your signature
- name - your printed name
- position - Marketing Assistant

Stage 3: Identify Relevant Information

- special intensive course for managers

- enclose brochure

- course developed because of Single Market

- contents:
  - importance of language training
  - trade policies of other countries
  - cultural differences

- date: October 10th - 15th 1992

- place: Grande Hotel, Black Street, London, W1

- cost: £100 per day per person

Now complete the following stages.

Stage 4: Group/Order Relevant Information

....
....
....
....
....
....
....
....
....

Letters

Stage 5: Write the Letter

Stage 6: Check your Work ☑

Checklist: Letter

1. Have you completed the task? ☐
2. Is your layout correct? ☐
3. Do you have all the correct information? ☐
4. Is it ordered in the best way? ☐
5. Is the language appropriate for a letter? ☐
6. Have you checked spelling, grammar and punctuation? ☐

SECTION 1

Practice 5

Situation: You are Geoff Pullar, Director of Personnel at Aegis Insurance Company. Next month the Managing Director, Dr Glen Turner, of your Australian branch is to visit the headquarters of your company for two days.

Task: Send a letter to him at Lake View Tower, 264 High Street, Allambie, NSW 2100, Australia, confirming the dates of his visit. Indicate who will meet him at the airport, where he will stay and a brief outline of his two-day programme.

Note: Lay out your answer as a **letter**. Make up any necessary details.

(Series 3, 1993, Q1)

Stage 1: Identify the Task

Write the letter.

Stage 2: Layout

- your company address - Aegis Insurance Company, 24 High Street, Newcastle, NE46 4AA, England
- the date - 30th June 1993
- the name and address of the person to whom you are writing - Dr Glen Turner, Aegis Insurance Company, Lake View Tower, 264 High Street, Allambie, NSW 2100, Australia
- the correct salutation - Dear Dr Turner
- complimentary close - Yours sincerely
- a signature - your signature
- name - Geoff Pullar
- position - Director of Personnel

Now complete the following stages.

Stage 3: Identify Relevant Information

Stage 4: Group/Order Relevant Information

Letters

Stage 5: Write the Letter

Stage 6: Check your Work ✓

Checklist: Letter

1. Have you completed the task? ☐
2. Is your layout correct? ☐
3. Do you have all the correct information? ☐
4. Is it ordered in the best way? ☐
5. Is the language appropriate for a letter? ☐
6. Have you checked spelling, grammar and punctuation? ☐

SECTION 1

Practice 6

Situation: As the Office Manager of a large fruit-packing company you have been asked to investigate the cost of a day's summer outing for both the office and the factory workers.

Task: Write a **letter** to a local coach company asking for a quotation for the hire of coaches for a day's excursion of your choice. Specify the number of people, the time of departure and return, and the destination.

Note: *Lay out your answer as a **letter**. Make up any necessary details.*

(Series 1, 1991, Q1)

Stage 1: Identify the Task
Write the letter.

Now complete the following stages.

Stage 2: Layout

your company address - ....

the date - ....

the name and address of person to whom you are writing - ....

....

the correct salutation - ....

complimentary close - ....

a signature/name/position - ....

Stage 3: Identify Relevant Information	Stage 4: Group/Order Relevant Information
....	....
....	....
....	....
....	....
....	....
....	....
....	....
....	....
....	....
....	....
....	....
....	....
....	....

Letters

Stage 5:   Write the Letter

Stage 6:   Check your Work

Checklist: Letter

1   Have you completed the task?
2   Is your layout correct?
3   Do you have all the correct information?
4   Is it ordered in the best way?
5   Is the language appropriate for a letter?
6   Have you checked spelling, grammar and punctuation?

SECTION 1

Practice 7

Situation: The annual European three-day Sales Conference for Regional Managers due to take place the week after next will have to be postponed due to unforeseen circumstances. Two of the speakers, Professor G MacDougal and John Delors, will not be able to attend. However, you have found two replacement speakers with different areas of specialisation.

Task: Write a **letter** to all Regional Managers apologising for the postponement, explaining the changes and confirming times and places. Make up any relevant details.

Now complete the following stages.

Stage 1: Identify the Task

....

Stage 2: Layout

your company address - ....

the date - ....

the name and address of person to whom you are writing - ....

....

the correct salutation - ....

complimentary close - ....

a signature/name/position - ....

Stage 3: Identify Relevant Information	Stage 4: Group/Order Relevant Information
....	....
....	....
....	....
....	....
....	....
....	....
....	....
....	....
....	....
....	....
....	....
....	....
....	....
....	....
....	....

Stage 5: Write the Letter

Stage 6: Check your Work ☑

Checklist: Letter

1 Have you completed the task? ☐
2 Is your layout correct? ☐
3 Do you have all the correct information? ☐
4 Is it ordered in the best way? ☐
5 Is the language appropriate for a letter? ☐
6 Have you checked spelling, grammar and punctuation? ☐

SECTION 1

Practice 8

Situation: You are looking for a new job. In your local newspaper you see two advertisements. Decide whether you should apply for a job as:
a secretary/receptionist
b a post in junior management
c an office post

SECRETARY/RECEPTIONIST

Applications are invited from persons aged 16-35 for this post. Applicants should have good typing speeds and other relevant office skills.

Apply in writing giving details of age, qualifications, work experience and the names and addresses of two referees to:

Mrs Y Edwards
The National Trust Company
2-10 Albert Street
Ashton
AS7 9EZ

Applicants should explain which aspects of the secretary's/receptionist's work they would find most interesting.

WANTED

JUNIOR MANAGEMENT
& OFFICE STAFF

Staff Selection & Co
2 Kennedy Road
Ashton
AS9 6TT

We have both temporary and permanent jobs for all types of junior management staff with a number of local and international companies. We also have a limited number of openings for office staff.

Write for further details, giving particulars of age, experience, qualifications and the names and addresses of two referees. Applicants should indicate the type of work which interests them most and the sort of company they would like to work for, with reasons.

Task: Choose the advertisement which is more relevant to you. Write an application letter in response to the advertisement you have chosen. You may use your own age and personal details or make up appropriate information. Set the letter out appropriately.

(Series 2, 1988, Q1)

Now complete the following stages.

Stage 1: Identify the Task

....

Stage 2: Layout

your company address - ....

....

the date - ....

the name and address of person to whom you are writing - ....

....

the correct salutation - ....

complimentary close - ....

a signature/name/position - ....

Stage 3: Identify Relevant Information	**Stage 4: Group/Order Relevant Information**
....	....
....	....
....	....
....	....
....	....
....	....
....	....
....	....
....	....
....	....
....	....
....	....
....	....
....	....

SECTION 1

Stage 5: Write the Letter

Stage 6: Check your Work ✓

Checklist: Letter

1 Have you completed the task? ☐
2 Is your layout correct? ☐
3 Do you have all the correct information? ☐
4 Is it ordered in the best way? ☐
5 Is the language appropriate for a letter? ☐
6 Have you checked spelling, grammar and punctuation? ☐

Practice 9

Situation: Mr Roderick MacDonald, Managing Director of Woomera Bio-Technics Pty, 1 Rockingham Way, Melbourne, Victoria, Australia is going to visit your company to discuss the possibility of producing some of Bio-Technics products in your factory. Unfortunately, you have just received a telephone call from your manager informing you that it is necessary to change Mr MacDonald's programme at short notice.

Task: Using the following notes you made when you received the telephone call, write a **letter** to Mr MacDonald. Explain what the changes are, why they have been made and apologise. Send a new programme with your letter. Make up the name and address of your own company and other necessary information.

Note: *Write the letter followed by the new programme.*
(Series 2, 1990, Q1)

Original Programme

Day 1   Flight arrival 1600.   Our driver will meet you and take you to the "Merlin Hotel".

Day 2   Leave hotel 0800.   Meeting at Head Office all day.

Day 3   Leave hotel 0800.   Tour of factory, with the Production Manager, finishing at 1400.

Day 4   Leave hotel 0800.   Tour of warehouse facilities, with the Warehouse Manager, finishing at 1200. Further meeting at Head Office, finishing at 1600.

Day 5   Leave hotel 0900.   Flight departure 1100.

Telephone Notes

Merlin Hotel no longer available (being refurbished). Room booked at "Camelot Hotel".

Camelot Hotel nearer so driver will call each day 45 minutes later than originally planned.

The warehouse tour and the factory tour will be on the same day, leaving day four free for a Head Office meeting that will finish after lunch. Give the names of the people Mr MacDonald will meet each day.

SECTION 1

Now complete the following stages.

Stage 1:   Identify the Task

....

....

Stage 2:   Layout

your company address - ....

....

the date - ....

the name and address of person to whom you are writing - ....

....

the correct salutation - ....

complimentary close - ....

a signature/name/position - ....

Stage 3:   Identify Relevant Information   **Stage 4:   Group/Order Relevant Information**

Letters

Stage 5: Write the Letter

Stage 6: Check your Work ☑

Checklist: Letter

1. Have you completed the task? ☐
2. Is your layout correct? ☐
3. Do you have all the correct information? ☐
4. Is it ordered in the best way? ☐
5. Is the language appropriate for a letter? ☐
6. Have you checked spelling, grammar and punctuation? ☐

SECTION 1

Practice 10

Situation: You are the assistant to the Personnel Manager of International Assets. Your company has four factories in Britain - one in the south, one in the west and two in the north. The one in the south is the oldest and the largest, but it makes little or no profit. Your company has decided to close the factory in the south and expand and modernise one of the factories in the north and the one in the west.

The company does not want to dismiss any employees. It hopes that its policies of *relocation* and early *retirement* will give jobs to people who want them, and will allow others to retire (see table below).

Task: Draft a **letter** from the Personnel Manager to all company employees. The letter should explain the company's plans for its factories and its workforce, using information from the table. **Set the letter out appropriately**, beginning "Dear Colleague". You may make up appropriate information but do not give unnecessary details.

(Series 4, 1989, Q1)

FACTORY	WORKFORCE		DIFFERENCE	TARGET	
	1990	1992		Relocation	Retirement
A (South)	10,000	0	-10,000	7,000	3,000
B (West)	6,000	10,000	+4,000	0	0
C (North)	6,000	10,000	+4,000	0	0
D (North)	8,000	6,000	-2,000	1,000	1,000

Letters

Now complete the following stages.

Stage 1: Identify the Task

....

Stage 2: Layout

your company address - ....

....

the date - ....

the name and address of person to whom you are writing - ....

....

the correct salutation - ....

complimentary close - ....

a signature/name/position - ....

Stage 3: Identify Relevant Information	**Stage 4: Group/Order Relevant Information**
....	....
....	....
....	....
....	....
....	....
....	....
....	....
....	....
....	....
....	....
....	....
....	....
....	....

SECTION 1

Stage 5: Write the Letter

Stage 6: Check your Work ☑

Checklist: Letter

1. Have you completed the task? ☐
2. Is your layout correct? ☐
3. Do you have all the correct information? ☐
4. Is it ordered in the best way? ☐
5. Is the language appropriate for a letter? ☐
6. Have you checked spelling, grammar and punctuation? ☐

SECTION 2: Memos

Introduction

Question 1 is always either a letter or a memo. This section looks at memos.

Stage 1: Identify the Task

Read the question and work out exactly what you are required to do. The instruction at the bottom of the question normally reads, "Lay your answer out as a memo" or "Set out the memo".

Stage 2: Layout

A memo should include the following information:

- Who is the memo to?
- Who is the memo from?
- What is the subject of the memo?
- What is the date?

These should be positioned as opposite:

> **MEMO**
>
> To:
> From:
> Subject:
> Date:

Stage 3: Identify Relevant Information

A memo is usually fairly short. It should include enough so that the correct information is communicated, but should not include anything extra to this.

Stage 4: Group/Order Relevant Information

Often the information in the question is presented in a suitable order. Sometimes, however, the different information may be mixed up. In this case it is useful to group information according to themes.

Stage 5: Write the Memo

Language in memos is shorter and more direct than in a letter. Stay to the point, but be polite. Be careful for extra instructions, eg questions which say "make up any necessary details".

Stage 6: Check your Work

Checklist: Memo

The following is a list of points to check when you write a memo.

1. Have you completed the task? (Will the person who receives the memo be able to understand the message?)
2. Is it to the correct person? Is it from the correct person? (Are you writing it under your name?)
3. Does the subject line describe the main content in a few words?
4. Is the date correct? (The day of writing.)
5. Have you included all relevant information? (Is any information missing which will hinder understanding of the message?)
6. Have you left out all irrelevant information?
7. Have you grouped/ordered information in the best way?
8. Is the language appropriate for a memo? (Not too polite, but not too short.)
9. Have you checked spelling, grammar and punctuation?

SECTION 2

Practice 1

Situation: You are the leader of a small section in your company. One of the people who works in the section, Miss Charlotte Lucas, recently wrote to the Personnel Manager requesting permission to have a week's leave to attend the wedding of a close relative in another country. Permission was refused. Miss Lucas has asked you to help her.

Task: Write a **memo** to the Personnel Manager, supporting Miss Lucas's request for a week's leave. Remember that you have to persuade him to reconsider his decision. Refer to the high quality of Miss Lucas's work, her length of service and good attendance record. Say how the section will manage without her and mention any other points which support your case.

Note: Lay out your answer as a memo, **not** a letter. Make up any necessary information.

(Series 3, 1990, Q1)

Stage 1: Identify the Task
Write the memo.

Stage 2: Layout

To: (make up name), Personnel Manager
From: (your name)
Subject: Miss Lucas's request for a week's leave
Date: (today's date)

Stage 3: Identify Relevant Information

- ref: Miss Charlotte Lucas's letter to you
- requesting week's leave
- wedding of close relative in another country
- permission refused
- Miss Lucas has asked me to help
- high quality of her work
- good attendance record
- recent flu epidemic, overtime to help
- length of service 15 years
- several times worked weekend to help out
- low workload in the requested week and staff happy to take on work
- important for her to attend wedding
- loyalty must be rewarded
- glad to help her
- reconsider decision

Stage 4: Group/Order Relevant Information

1. Ref: Miss Charlotte Lucas.
2. Letter requesting week's leave.
3. Wedding of close relative in another country.
4. Permission refused.
5. Miss Lucas has asked me to help.
6. Do this gladly.
7. Length of service 15 years.
8. Miss Lucas has a very good attendance record.
9. High quality of work.
10. Recent flu epidemic, overtime to help.
11. Several times worked weekend to help out.
12. Loyalty must be rewarded.
13. Workload not too heavy in the week requested and other staff are always happy to take on her work to help out.
14. Very important for Miss Lucas to attend the wedding.
15. Reconsider decision.

Stage 5: Write the Memo

MEMO

To: (make up name), Personnel Manager
From: (your name)
Subject: Miss Lucas's request for a week's leave
Date: (today's date)

Recently Miss Charlotte Lucas, from my section, wrote to you requesting a week's leave to attend the wedding of a close relative in another country. A request which was refused. Miss Lucas has asked for my help, which I am glad to offer.

Miss Lucas has been with the company over 15 years and has an almost 100% attendance record. Her work is of the highest quality and she is always willing to help out. During a recent flu epidemic she worked many overtime hours so that the department did not fall behind with its work and on several occasions she has worked at weekends for no pay, just to help. This loyalty must be rewarded, especially as in the week she requested our workload will not be too heavy and can be easily covered by other members of staff, who have already offered to take on her work.

This wedding is very important for Miss Lucas and I ask you to reconsider your decision.

Stage 6: Check your Work ☑

Checklist: Memo

1. Have you completed the task?
2. Is it to the correct person? Is it from the correct person? ☑
3. Does the subject line tell you in a few words what the memo is about? ☑
4. Is it the correct date? ☑
5. Have you included all relevant information? ☑
6. Have you left out all irrelevant information? ☑
7. Have you ordered the information in the best way? ☑
8. Is the language appropriate for a memo? ☑
9. Have you checked spelling, grammar and punctuation? ☑

SECTION 2

Practice 2

Situation: Your Manager, Mr Schmidt, has asked you to send a memorandum on an accident that happened in the office recently. You have spoken to the injured person and others, and read the official accident report form (see below).

Task: **Write the memo to Mr Schmidt**, explain how and why the accident happened and suggest ways of preventing such accidents from happening in future.

Note: *Lay out your answer as a memo, **not** a letter. Make up any necessary information.*
(Series 4, 1990, Q1)

injury – Schädigung / Verletzung
attempt – Versuchen / Versuch

ACCIDENT REPORT FORM

Date of accident:	Thursday 5 June	Time of accident:	2.20pm
Location:	Photocopying Room	Person injured:	Miss Elizabeth Bennett a trainee in the Sales Department
Nature of injury:	Broken arm, cuts and bruises. *(Quetschung / Hämatom)*		
Details of accident:	Miss Bennett fell from a chair while attempting to lift a box of photocopy paper from a high shelf. She was operating the machine herself as the person whose job it is had not returned from lunch.		
Was injured person taken to hospital?	Yes		
How long will injured person be off work?	At least three weeks.		

Stage 1: Identify the Task
Write the memo.

Stage 2: Layout
To: Mr Schmidt
From: (your name)
Subject: Accident of Miss Bennett / Preventative measures to be taken
Date: 10 June

Stage 3: Identify Relevant Information
- accident happened on 5 June
- Miss Elizabeth Bennett - trainee - Sales Department
- fell off chair while lifting box off shelf
- operating machine herself
- operator not back from lunch
- in future, photocopy paper kept on floor near to the photocopier
- fixed times for using photocopier when operator there
- members of staff not allowed to photocopy
- organise a seminar on "Accident Prevention"

Stage 4: Group/Order Relevant Information
1. Accident happened on 5 June.
2. Miss Elizabeth Bennett - trainee - Sales Department.
3. Fell off chair while lifting box off shelf.
4. Operating machine herself.
5. Operator not back from lunch.
6. In future, photocopy paper kept on floor near to the photocopier.
7. Fixed times for using photocopier when operator there.
8. Members of staff not allowed to photocopy.
9. Organise a seminar on "Accident Prevention".

Stage 5: Write the Memo

MEMO

To: Mr Schmidt

From: (your name)

Subject: Accident of Miss Bennett / Preventative measures to be taken

Date: 10 June

The accident happened on 5 June when Miss Elizabeth Bennett, a trainee in the Sales Department, fell off a chair whilst trying to lift a heavy box of photocopy paper down off a high shelf. Miss Bennett was operating the machine herself as the person responsible was still on their lunch break.

To avoid accidents in the future the photocopy paper is to be kept on the floor near to the photocopier and we have introduced fixed times for photocopying, when the operator will be present. Members of staff are not allowed to do their own photocopying.

We have also arranged to hold a seminar on Accident Prevention.

Now complete the following stage.

Stage 6: Check your Work

Checklist: Memo

1. Have you completed the task? ☐
2. Is it to the correct person? Is it from the correct person? ☐
3. Does the subject line tell you in a few words what the memo is about? ☐
4. Is it the correct date? ☐
5. Have you included all relevant information? ☐
6. Have you left out all irrelevant information? ☐
7. Have you ordered the information in the best way? ☐
8. Is the language appropriate for a memo? ☐
9. Have you checked spelling, grammar and punctuation? ☐

SECTION 2

trial period - Testphase
appropriate - zuweisen, relevant, passend
objection - Einwand

Practice 3

Situation: Some people in your company have asked for smoking to be banned from office areas. At a recent meeting of staff and management it was decided to send a questionnaire to all employees to find out everyone's opinion.

Task: You are Office Manager. Send a **memo** to all employees, explain:

    a   why some people object to smoking in the offices
    b   the decision of the recent meeting
    c   the purpose of the questionnaire
    d   that there will be a trial period based on the results of the questionnaire (beginning on the first of next month)
    e   how long the trial period will last
    f   that the final decision on a smoking policy will be made at the end of the trial period

Include a **tear-off slip** at the bottom of your memo. There should be spaces for the following information: employee's name
        employee's choice (total ban on smoking/non-smoking areas/complete freedom)

Tell colleagues how to return their slips to you.

Note: *You may also use your own personal details or make up appropriate information.* **Set the memo out appropriately.**

(Series 2, 1989, Q1)

Stage 1: Identify the Task
Write a memo.

Stage 2: Layout
To: All employees
From: (your name)
Subject: Smoking in offices
Date: (today's date)

Stage 3: Identify Relevant Information
- recent staff/management meeting
- decision to find out everyone's opinion on smoking in offices
- send questionnaire
- objections - unpleasant/dirty
- questionnaire to decide what to do
- trial period based on results
- length 3 months
- end of trial period/final decision
- tear-off slip for name and opinion
- return to Mr J Brown, Room 321, a s a p

Stage 4: Group/Order Relevant Information
1. Objections to smoking - unpleasant and dirty.
2. Recent staff/management meeting.
3. Decision to find out everyone's opinion.
4. Send out questionnaire.
5. Tear-off slips for name and opinion.
6. Trial period based on results.
7. Length 3 months.
8. End of trial period will give final decision.
9. Return to Mr J Brown, Room 321, a s a p.

Now complete the following stages.

Stage 5: Write the Memo

Stage 6: Check your Work ✓

Checklist: Memo

1. Have you completed the task? ☐
2. Is it to the correct person? Is it from the correct person? ☐
3. Does the subject line tell you in a few words what the memo is about? ☐
4. Is it the correct date? ☐
5. Have you included all relevant information? ☐
6. Have you left out all irrelevant information? ☐
7. Have you ordered the information in the best way? ☐
8. Is the language appropriate for a memo? ☐
9. Have you checked spelling, grammar and punctuation? ☐

SECTION 2

Practice 4

Situation: The staff restaurant on the fourth floor of your office block is to be closed for one week for re-decoration.

Task: As Catering Manager you are to send a **memo** to the Office Manager, Peter MacParland, explaining why the restaurant is to close and for how long. Specify what alternative arrangements will be made for providing drinks and snacks during the morning and afternoon breaks, and providing meals at lunch times.

Note: *Lay out your answer as a **memo**. Make up any necessary details.*
(Series 1, 1993, Q1)

Stage 1: Identify the Task

Write the memo.

Stage 2: Layout

To: Peter MacParland, Office Manager
From: (your name), Catering Manager
Subject: Closure of staff restaurant
Date: (today's date)

Stage 3: Identify Relevant Information

- restaurant closed for one week, from next Monday
- re-decoration
- catering firm will sell drinks and sandwiches during morning and afternoon breaks
- near reception, first floor
- lunches provided at Rafters Restaurant in the High Street
- open 12pm - 1pm
- special menu for employees at usual prices

Now complete the following stages.

Stage 4: Group/Order Relevant Information

....
....
....
....
....
....
....

Memos

Stage 5: Write the Memo

Stage 6: Check your Work

Checklist: Memo

1. Have you completed the task? ☐
2. Is it to the correct person? Is it from the correct person? ☐
3. Does the subject line tell you in a few words what the memo is about? ☐
4. Is it the correct date? ☐
5. Have you included all relevant information? ☐
6. Have you left out all irrelevant information? ☐
7. Have you ordered the information in the best way? ☐
8. Is the language appropriate for a memo? ☐
9. Have you checked spelling, grammar and punctuation? ☐

SECTION 2

Practice 5

Situation: The monthly photocopying bill for your company has recently increased enormously. As Office Manager, you must do something about this, but at the moment it is impossible to check how many photocopies each employee is making each month. You have decided to fit a "Copyguard" to the photocopier. This is a small computer which keeps a record of how many photocopies each employee makes. Each employee will have a six-figure personal access number and this must be typed into the "Copyguard" in order to switch the photocopier on. The photocopier will not work if the access number is not typed into the "Copyguard" and so anyone without a number will not be able to use it.

Task: Write a **memo** to all employees. Include the following information in your memo:
- a An explanation of the problem with the photocopier.
- b Your views on the cause of this problem.
- c What you are doing to overcome this problem.
- d A brief explanation of how the system will work.
- e Details of when the next system will come into operation.
- f A tear-off slip at the bottom of the memo for employees to return to you. This must show the employee's name, job and the six-figure access number they have chosen.

Note: Set the memo out appropriately, using today's date. You should make up other useful information (eg photocopying totals).

(Series 3, 1988, Q1)

Stage 1: Identify the Task
Write the memo.

Stage 2: Layout
To: All employees
From: (your name), Office Manager
Subject: Photocopying and "Copyguard"
Date: (today's date)

Now complete the following stages.

Stage 3: Identify Relevant Information

Stage 4: Group/Order Relevant Information

Memos

Stage 5: Write the Memo

Stage 6: Check your Work ☑

Checklist: Memo

1. Have you completed the task? ☐
2. Is it to the correct person? Is it from the correct person? ☐
3. Does the subject line tell you in a few words what the memo is about? ☐
4. Is it the correct date? ☐
5. Have you included all relevant information? ☐
6. Have you left out all irrelevant information? ☐
7. Have you ordered the information in the best way? ☐
8. Is the language appropriate for a memo? ☐
9. Have you checked spelling, grammar and punctuation? ☐

SECTION 2

Practice 6

Situation: At a staff meeting last week it was decided for environmental reasons to save waste paper for recycling.

Task: As Office Manager you are to send a **memo** to the Managing Director, Frank Chadburn, explaining what was decided and why. You should also give **brief** details of where containers are to be placed in your three-storey office block, and when and by whom they are to be collected.

Note: *Lay out your answer as a memo*. Make up any necessary details.

(Series 2, 1992, Q1)

Stage 1: Identify the Task

Write the memo.

Now complete the following stages.

Stage 2: Layout

To: ....
From: ....
Subject: ....
Date: ....

Stage 3: Identify Relevant Information

Stage 4: Group/Order Relevant Information

Memos

Stage 5: Write the Memo

Stage 6: Check your Work ☑

Checklist: Memo

1. Have you completed the task? ☐
2. Is it to the correct person? Is it from the correct person? ☐
3. Does the subject line tell you in a few words what the memo is about? ☐
4. Is it the correct date? ☐
5. Have you included all relevant information? ☐
6. Have you left out all irrelevant information? ☐
7. Have you ordered the information in the best way? ☐
8. Is the language appropriate for a memo? ☐
9. Have you checked spelling, grammar and punctuation? ☐

SECTION 2

Practice 7

Situation: You work for a large manufacturing company in the capital of your country. Mr J Ruru, an executive of your company's branch in Indonesia, is visiting Head Office in your country. You have to arrange the details of his programme for tomorrow. He has asked to visit one of the company's main suppliers. Their factory is about 100 kilometres (60 miles) from the capital.

Task: Write a **memo** to Mr Ruru, giving the following information:

a Details of the company he is visiting - name, brief information of its value to your company, time of meeting, the people he is meeting, etc.

b Details of the transport you have arranged for him - how he is to travel, time he must leave his hotel, expected time of return etc.

c Suggestions for an evening out in the capital for him - such as restaurant or theatre visit with appropriate directions and transport advice.

Note: *Set out the memo appropriately, using tomorrow's date. You should make up other appropriate information (names of companies, your position, etc).*

(Series 4, 1988, Q1)

Now complete the following stages.

Stage 1: Identify the Task

....

....

Stage 2: Layout

To: ....
From: ....
Subject: ....
Date: ....

Stage 3: Identify Relevant Information

Stage 4: Group/Order Relevant Information

Stage 5: Write the Memo

Stage 6: Check your Work ✓

Checklist: Memo

1. Have you completed the task? ☐
2. Is it to the correct person? Is it from the correct person? ☐
3. Does the subject line tell you in a few words what the memo is about? ☐
4. Is it the correct date? ☐
5. Have you included all relevant information? ☐
6. Have you left out all irrelevant information? ☐
7. Have you ordered the information in the best way? ☐
8. Is the language appropriate for a memo? ☐
9. Have you checked spelling, grammar and punctuation? ☐

SECTION 2

Practice 8

Situation: You are the Manager of a large branch of a nation-wide insurance company. Various members of staff have started arriving late in the mornings, causing inconvenience to customers and some bad feeling among those employees who arrive on time.

Task: Send a **memo** to your section leaders explaining the situation and the problems it is causing and telling them to take appropriate action to re-establish punctuality.

Note: *Lay out your answer as a memo, **not** a letter. Make up any necessary details.*
(Series 4, 1991, Q1)

Now complete the following stages.

Stage 1: Identify the Task

....

Stage 2: Layout

To: ....
From: ....
Subject: ....
Date: ....

Stage 3: Identify Relevant Information   **Stage 4: Group/Order Relevant Information**

Memos

Stage 5: Write the Memo

Stage 6: Check your Work ☑

Checklist: Memo

1. Have you completed the task? ☐
2. Is it to the correct person? Is it from the correct person? ☐
3. Does the subject line tell you in a few words what the memo is about? ☐
4. Is it the correct date? ☐
5. Have you included all relevant information? ☐
6. Have you left out all irrelevant information? ☐
7. Have you ordered the information in the best way? ☐
8. Is the language appropriate for a memo? ☐
9. Have you checked spelling, grammar and punctuation? ☐

SECTION 2

Practice 9

Situation: You are the Office Manager of a large insurance company which occupies four floors of an office block. The canteen is in the basement and twice a day four ladies walk around the building with a trolley of coffee, tea and biscuits. It has been decided to replace these tea ladies with vending machines - two on each floor - to enable employees to have drinks when they want.

Task: Write a **memo** to all staff explaining the decision, giving reasons and also explaining that the tea ladies will not lose their jobs. You should also emphasise the fact that the vending machines will also make available soft drinks.

Note: *Lay out your answer as a memo. Make up any necessary details.*
(Series 2, 1991, Q1)

Now complete the following stages.

Stage 1: Identify the Task

....

Stage 2: Layout

To: ....
From: ....
Subject: ....
Date: ....

Stage 3: Identify Relevant Information	Stage 4: Group/Order Relevant Information
....	....
....	....
....	....
....	....
....	....
....	....
....	....
....	....
....	....
....	....
....	....
....	....
....	....
....	....

Memos

Stage 5: Write the Memo

Stage 6: Check your Work ☑

Checklist: Memo

1. Have you completed the task? ☐
2. Is it to the correct person? Is it from the correct person? ☐
3. Does the subject line tell you in a few words what the memo is about? ☐
4. Is it the correct date? ☐
5. Have you included all relevant information? ☐
6. Have you left out all irrelevant information? ☐
7. Have you ordered the information in the best way? ☐
8. Is the language appropriate for a memo? ☐
9. Have you checked spelling, grammar and punctuation? ☐

SECTION 2

Practice 10

Situation: The Chairman of the company for which you work is to pay a visit to your London offices next week. He is very keen on appearances.

Task: You are the Office Manager of the four-storey London office block. Send a **memo** to the Chief Caretaker, Ralph Charrer, informing him of the forthcoming visit and instructing him to ensure that the building is in a good state to be "inspected". Mention in particular the reception area and the staff restaurant, among others.

Note: *Lay out your answer as a memo. Make up any necessary details.*
(Series 1, 1992, Q1)

Now complete the following stages.

Stage 1: Identify the Task

....

Stage 2: Layout

To: ....
From: ....
Subject: ....
Date: ....

Stage 3: Identify Relevant Information	Stage 4: Group/Order Relevant Information
....	....
....	....
....	....
....	....
....	....
....	....
....	....
....	....
....	....
....	....
....	....
....	....

Stage 5: Write the Memo

Stage 6: Check your Work ☑

Checklist: Memo

1. Have you completed the task? ☐
2. Is it to the correct person? Is it from the correct person? ☐
3. Does the subject line tell you in a few words what the memo is about? ☐
4. Is it the correct date? ☐
5. Have you included all relevant information? ☐
6. Have you left out all irrelevant information? ☐
7. Have you ordered the information in the best way? ☐
8. Is the language appropriate for a memo? ☐
9. Have you checked spelling, grammar and punctuation? ☐

SECTION 2

SECTION 3: Short Answers

Introduction

The type of question requiring short answers may occur in Question 2 or in Question 3.

Stage 1: Identify the Task

There is often a lot of text/information in this question. Before you start to read this, look at the instructions carefully to see exactly what you have to do and what kind of answers are required. Instructions often say "Answer the question briefly but precisely" or "Your answers should be brief."

Stage 2: How to Complete the Task

When you have read through the task, do not panic when you see a lot of text. It is as important to be able to pick out specific information as to ignore irrelevant information from the authentic piece of text given. You are also asked to answer specific questions only, so do not panic if you find a lot of new words. Try and guess what they mean. If you can't, ignore them.

The best approach is:

1 Read all the questions first.
2 Read all the text before answering any questions.
3 Read the questions one at a time and look for specific answers.

Remember:

- the information in the text is not always in the same order as in the questions
- make sure you give the information you are asked for
- if you can't answer a question, go on to the next and come back to it later

Stage 3: How to Answer

If it is possible to answer with one word or a number then do so. If more information is required, keep it as brief as possible.

Stage 4: Check your Work

Checklist: Short Answers

The following is a list of points to check when you give short answers.

1 Have you completed the task?
2 Have you answered as briefly as possible?
3 Have you answered all the questions?
4 Have you checked spelling, grammar and punctuation?

SECTION 3

Practice 1

Situation: A colleague has asked you to check some details of cheap flights.

Task: Use the information below, taken from a leisure magazine, to answer the questions below briefly but precisely. Do **not** write on the question paper. Write **only** the answers in your answer book.

(Series 1, 1993, Q3)

Stage 1: Identify the Task

Answer the questions briefly but precisely.

Stage 2: Before you Start

Have you read through **all** the questions?
Have you read through **all** the information?

Questions

1. Do the prices quoted include accommodation?
2. Does Aztec Travel deal with charter flights?
3. From which airport do I depart on the flight to Amsterdam?
4. How many companies could I contact for the cheap flight to New York?
5. How often does this guide appear?
6. In what currency are the fares quoted?
7. Is the flight to Hong Kong non-stop?
8. Is there unlimited availability on the charter flights?
9. What number do I call for the cheap flight to Casablanca?
10. Which company has the cheapest flight to Geneva?

Flight Box Key

AT   Aztec Travel (081 852 7961)

CDD   Crowe, Drydale, Deatin (081 318 5633)

RBA   Richard Blane Associates (071 633 1942)

TC   Travel Co (071 291 0861)

*   Booking restrictions

Seats at these prices were available at the time of going to press.

Flight Box   A weekly feature giving an at-a-glance guide to the cheapest 'flight-only' deals on popular holiday routes.

Destination (UK Airport)	Cheapest Fare £	Available From	Airline	Destination (UK Airport)	Cheapest Fare £	Available From	Airline
Geneva (Heathrow)	98	CDD	Scheduled	Tenerife (Gatwick)	89	AT	Charter*
Paris (Heathrow)	80	AT/TC	Scheduled	Casablanca (Heathrow)	115	RBA	Scheduled
Amsterdam (Gatwick)	87	RBA	Scheduled	Rome (Heathrow)	140	CDD	Scheduled
New York (Heathrow)	200	CDD/TC	Scheduled	Hong Kong (Heathrow via Dubai)	475	AT	Scheduled
Orlando (Gatwick)	233	TC	Charter*	Sydney (Heathrow via Colombo)	630	CDD	Scheduled

Short Answers

Stage 3: Write the Answers

1. No

2. Yes

3. Gatwick

4. Two

5. Weekly

6. £ Sterling

7. No

8. No

9. 071 633 1942

10. Crowe, Drydale, Deatin

Stage 4: Check your Work ☑

Checklist: Short Answers

1	Have you completed the task?	
2	Have you answered as briefly as possible?	☑
3	Have you answered all the questions?	☑
4	Have you checked spelling, grammar and punctuation?	☑

SECTION 3

Practice 2

Situation: You work in the library of a fruit import company and the Board wants some information about the situation in Spain.

Task: Use the short magazine extract below to answer the questions below **briefly** but **precisely**.

(Series 2, 1993, Q2)

Stage 1: Identify the Task
Answer the questions briefly but precisely.

Stage 2: Before you Start
Have you read through **all** the questions?
Have you read through **all** the information?

Worried Spanish lemon growers have set up a special commission to try to solve the problems of a declining market and competition from non-EC countries, in both Europe and South America.

This move comes after exports last year fell by 33,000 tonnes, leaving an estimated 69,000 tonnes of fruit on the trees. In the same period countries like Turkey - selling in the winter - and Argentina - selling during the summer - have increased their volumes from 40,000 to 55,000 tonnes.

The Spanish organisation has 15 members, drawn from industry associations, co-operatives and the trade in the Murcia and Valencia regions, which produce almost 90% of the total Spanish crop. Jaime T Iglesias, the co-ordinator of the commission said, at a press conference in Nuevo Castillo, that it will co-operate with other sectors, in particular the orange growers and the olive producers, but that it will hold independent views.

Although not yet legally recognised, the commission has already drawn up a series of measures. These include proposals to extend the season, cut production costs and improve quality. On the marketing side it has called for lemons to be included in the CAP (Common Agricultural Policy) with Community preference. It also wants an EC promotional campaign.

Its recommendations will be presented to the Spanish Ministry of Agriculture and the Andalusian Government in the next few weeks.

Questions

1 How many members make up the commission?
2 What do the initials CAP stand for?
3 What happened to the export of the Spanish lemons last year?
4 What have the Spanish lemon growers established?
5 Who is the co-ordinator of the commission?
6 In addition to marketing, what other measure(s) is the commission proposing?
7 What is the legal status of the commission?
8 Which competitors of the Spaniards are mentioned?
9 With which groups will the commission co-operate?
10 Who is to hear the recommendations?

Short Answers

Stage 3: Write the Answers

1. 15

2. Common Agricultural Policy

3. It fell

4. A special commission

5. Jaime T Iglesias

6. Extend the season/Cut production costs/Improve quality

7. Not yet legally recognised

8. Turkey/Argentina

9. Orange growers/Olive producers

10. The Spanish Ministry of Agriculture/The Andalusian Government

Now complete the following stage.

Stage 4: Check your Work ☑

Checklist: Short Answers

1. Have you completed the task? ☐
2. Have you answered as briefly as possible? ☐
3. Have you answered all the questions? ☐
4. Have you checked spelling, grammar and punctuation? ☐

SECTION 3

Practice 3

Situation: As a clerk in the enquiries section of the Post Office, you have been asked to familiarise yourself with the SwiftAir service in order to answer customers' queries.

Task: Use the information opposite to answer the following questions about the SwiftAir service.
(Series 1, 1991, Q2)

Stage 1: Identify the Task
Answer the questions briefly but precisely.

Stage 2: Before you Start
Have you read through **all** the questions?
Have you read through **all** the information?

Questions

1. How much more does SwiftAir cost than the normal Air Mail service?
2. Where can you buy single SwiftPacks?
3. How much does a certificate of posting cost?
4. How do you find out about contract facilities?
5. (a) Does a SwiftAir item travel with the normal mail?
   (b) What happens at each handling point?
6. What happens at an international sorting office?
7. How big are SwiftPacks?
8. When does a C2/CP3 form have to be used?
9. What labels have to be put on an item for it to receive the SwiftAir service?
10. What do you do if a SwiftPack is heavier than 60gms?
11. Where can you buy SwiftPacks in bulk?
12. In which two ways can you find out about discounts for bulk orders?
13. In what ways does the SwiftAir service differ from a courier service?

Short Answers

When you need to send important mail abroad **SwiftAir** is the express airmail service that ensures that your letters, papers or documents will arrive safely and economically.

Here's How it Works

SwiftAir is a priority letter service from the Royal Mail which means that it has access to a vast international network of postal collection and delivery channels. This means that SwiftAir items travel with the normal mail but at each handling point SwiftAir mail receives special treatment, speeding its sorting, and onwards dispatch.

On arrival at one of our five international sorting offices, SwiftAir items are immediately transferred and separately processed. They are then expressed to their destination on the first available flight, even on the day of posting, whenever possible.

Economy

Because SwiftAir mail travels within the international postal network it does not incur the high delivery costs of an expensive courier service. In this way SwiftAir provides an economical - as well as effective - alternative for all those times when you don't need a guaranteed ultra high speed delivery.

Simplicity

Just take your letter or packet to the Post Office, add stamps to the value of the normal airmail postage plus £1.85 then affix the **red** SwiftAir express label together with the **blue** Air Mail label and leave the rest to us. If you have a regular collection at your office, simply include your SwiftAir items in that, separated from other mail by an elastic band. Alternatively if the mail you are sending fits into a standard DL (10cm x 21.5cm), C5 (16.5cm x 23cm) or C4 (23cm x 33cm) envelope why not use one of our SwiftPacks?

SwiftPacks

SwiftPacks are a completely pre-paid envelope for items up to 60gms in weight and can be sent to anywhere in the world. You can purchase them singly at your Post Office counter or by mail order from the address shown in this leaflet.

Additional Benefits

Whether you use the SwiftAir service or convenient SwiftPacks you can register or insure your SwiftAir items to most countries (see Postal Rates, Overseas Leaflet) and a certificate of posting is available, free of charge, on request.

Contract Service

If you use SwiftAir on a regular basis why not take advantage of our contract facilities to make your express mailings even simpler. Phone 0800 581960 for further details.

Merchandise

When sending merchandise by SwiftAir all items must carry the green douane C1 label. If the value of the merchandise is over £270 then a C2/CP3 form must be used. Both of these can be obtained at Post Office counters.

Weight Limits

Small Packets	1kg
Letters or Printed Papers	2kg
Certain Books & Pamphlets*	5kg

See "Post Office Guide" for details.

* Australia, Bhutan, Bolivia, Colombia, Cuba, Myanmar (formerly Burma) and Papua New Guinea will only accept Small Packets up to 500gms.

SwiftPack Prices

SwiftPacks are available in 3 sizes from your local Post Office at the following prices:

DL (10cm x 21.5cm)	£2.25
C5 (16.5cm x 23cm)	£2.30
C4 (23cm x 33cm)	£2.35

And don't forget, that is fully pre-paid to anywhere in the world for 60gms weight. If the weight you enclose is over 60gms you simply add stamps to the value of this extra postage.

Mail Order Service

If you require a stock of SwiftPacks they are available in multiples of 10. Just send your cheque, made payable to "The Post Office" with your order to:

SwiftPacks
Freepost
The Publicity Centre
Fenton Way
Basildon
Essex
SS15 4BR

No stamp required.

Mail Order Prices

Pack of 10

DL envelopes	£22.50
C5 envelopes	£23.00
C4 envelopes	£23.50

Discounts are available for larger quantities. Please write to the address above for details or phone 0800 581960.

SwiftAir is a priority letter service **not** a guaranteed courier service.

SECTION 3

Now complete the following stages.

Stage 3: Write the Answers

Stage 4: Check your Work ✓

Checklist: Short Answers

1. Have you completed the task? ☐
2. Have you answered as briefly as possible? ☐
3. Have you answered all the questions? ☐
4. Have you checked spelling, grammar and punctuation? ☐

Short Answers

Practice 4

Situation: Your company is thinking of investing in Denmark and you have been asked to advise on Denmark's economic status for investment.

Task: To assist your research use the information in the advertisement on the next page to answer the questions below. Do **not** include irrelevant details. Write the answers in your answer book.

(Series 4, 1992, Q3)

Stage 1: Identify the Task

Answer the questions briefly but precisely.

Now complete the following stages.

Stage 2: Before you Start

Have you .... ?

Have you .... ?

Questions

1. Does Denmark belong to the EC?
2. Did Denmark rise on the Business Confidence Scoreboard in 1991?
3. Is the Danish Krone part of the European Monetary System?
4. Does Denmark have strong trade links with the Baltic States?
5. Does the Ministry of Economic Affairs forecast a rise in industrial exports for 1992?
6. Which European countries were rated above Denmark on the Business Confidence Scoreboard?
7. Did Sweden have a higher or lower rating than Denmark?
8. Which Latin countries were rated below Sweden and France?
9. Which ways does the advertisement suggest for obtaining information about investing in Denmark?
10. What % growth in GDP does the Ministry of Economic Affairs forecast for 1992?
11. How many European countries have a lower inflation rate than Denmark?
12. Were wage increases in other European countries in 1991 lower than Denmark?
13. How many foreign-owned companies, established in Denmark, have taken advantage of ties with Eastern Europe?
14. Was foreign investment in Denmark in 1988 above 1,000 million US $?
15. How many consumers exist in the European Community?

SECTION 3

What Businessmen think about Denmark

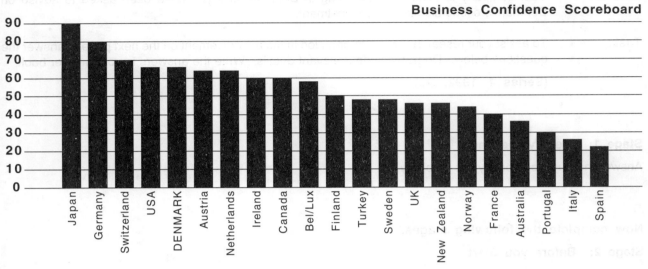

A steady rise in business confidence.

Business opinion about Denmark is changing. In 1991, the nation again improved its standing on the Business Confidence Scoreboard, climbing from 6th to 5th place.

A Strong Economy

Consider the economic picture. Denmark now has:

- The lowest inflation rate in Europe: less than 3%.
- A substantial and growing surplus in its balance of trade: more than 6% of GDP.
- Wage increases significantly below those of other European countries.
- A strong, stable currency tied to the European Monetary System.
- One of the lowest effective corporate tax rates in Europe.
- A reassuring economic outlook. For 1992, the Ministry of Economic Affairs projects:
  - a 2% improvement in competitiveness
  - a 6% increase in industrial exports and growth of 2.5% - 3% in GDP.

A Central Location

Denmark is also strategically located. As a member of the European Community, it has access to the 340 million consumers in the Single Market, and as a Scandinavian nation, it serves as a bridge to the non EC - but very affluent - Nordic countries.

There are also strong commercial links between Denmark and the new market economies of Eastern Europe, including the Baltic states. Foreign owned companies established in Denmark can take advantage of these ties. Indeed, some 2,000 firms are doing so right now, and the pace of direct foreign investment has increased markedly in recent years.

Businessmen are thinking about Denmark and perhaps you should too. For more information please contact the Ministry of Foreign Affairs or the Danish Embassy or Consulate General in your country.

SOURCE: Central Bank of Denmark, 1991

Foreign investment in Denmark continues to grow.

Short Answers

Stage 3: Write the Answers

Stage 4: Check your Work ☑

Checklist: Short Answers
1. Have you completed the task? ☐
2. Have you answered as briefly as possible? ☐
3. Have you answered all the questions? ☐
4. Have you checked spelling, grammar and punctuation? ☐

SECTION 3

Practice 5

Situation: Opposite there is the timetable for a management course you are due to attend.

Task: Study the timetable and answer the following questions. You should give specific times, days and week where necessary. Number your answers to refer to the questions.

(Series 1, 1992, Q3)

Now complete the following stages.

Stage 1: Identify the Task

....

Stage 2: Before you Start

Have you .... ?

Have you .... ?

Questions

1. When does the first simulation take place?

2. When does the course finish?

3. Will there be time for an evaluation of the course?

4. When is the third double session on Manufacturing?

5. Is the afternoon coffee break at the same time every day?

6. When is the last session on Personnel?

7. How many single sessions are available during the course for work on the Project before presentation?

8. When is the last session on Marketing?

9. How much time in total is timetabled for presentation of the projects? When?

10. When does the group exercise take place?

Short Answers

	WEEK ONE					
	MONDAY	**TUESDAY**	**WEDNESDAY**	**THURSDAY**	**FRIDAY**	**SATURDAY**
08.30 - 10.00	Tests and Needs Analysis	P1	P2	M1	M2	Simulation (09.00 - 12.30)
10.00 - 10.15	COFFEE BREAK					
10.15 - 11.15	—————————————— Self-Study ——————————————					
11.15 - 12.45	Group Exercise	S1	S2	BK1	S3	
	LUNCH					
13.45 - 14.45	MF1 d	1-1 or Self-Study	MF3 d	1-1 or Self-Study	BK2 d	
14.45 - 15.45	MF1	1-1 or Self-Study	MF3	1-1 or Self-Study	BK3	
15.45 - 16.00	COFFEE BREAK					
16.00 - 17.00	1-1 or Self-Study	MF2 d	1-1 or Self-Study	MF4 d	1-1 or Self-Study	
17.00 - 18.00	1-1 or Self-Study	MF2	1-1 or Self-Study	MF4	1-1 or Self-Study	

	WEEK TWO				
	MONDAY	**TUESDAY**	**WEDNESDAY**	**THURSDAY**	**FRIDAY**
08.30 - 10.00	Project	Project	Simulation - 1a	Students' Choice	MF7 (08.30 - 10.30)
10.00 - 10.15	COFFEE BREAK				
10.15 - 11.15	Self-Study	Self-Study	Self-Study	Self-Study	1-1 or Self-Study (10.45 - 12.45)
11.15 - 12.45	MF5	MF6	Simulation - 1b	Students' Choice	
	LUNCH				
13.45 - 14.45	PR1	PR3	1-1 or Self-Study	1-1 or Self-Study	Project Presentations
14.45 - 15.45	PR2	PR4	1-1 or Self-Study	1-1 or Self-Study	Project Presentations
15.45 - 16.00	COFFEE BREAK				
16.00 - 17.00	1-1 or Self-Study	1-1 or Self-Study	Project d	Project d	Project Presentations
17.00 - 18.00	1-1 or Self-Study	1-1 or Self-Study	Project	Project	Evaluation

Key to Abbreviations S Sales   PR Public Relations   M Marketing   MF Manufacturing
                         P Personnel   BK Book Keeping   d Double Session

SECTION 3

Stage 3: Write the Answers

Stage 4: Check your Work

Checklist: Short Answers

1   Have you completed the task? ☐
2   Have you answered as briefly as possible? ☐
3   Have you answered all the questions? ☐
4   Have you checked spelling, grammar and punctuation? ☐

Short Answers

Practice 6

Situation: Some business colleagues from overseas ask you how they can make international calls when they are in the UK. Since you have a leaflet about international calls, you are able to answer their questions.

Task: Read the leaflet on the next page and write down the answers that you give to the following questions. Your answers should be brief, but give all the information required.

(Series 3, 1990, Q2)

Now complete the following stages.

Stage 1: Identify the Task

....

Stage 2: Before you Start

Have you .... ?

Have you .... ?

Questions

1. How many ways are there of making an International call?
2. What does ICC stand for?
3. How many countries can be dialled direct?
4. What does IDD stand for?
5. Are phone cards only available at Post Offices?
6. Are the services you describe available on all British Telecom phones?
7. How much cash do I need to make an international call from a pay phone?
8. If I dial 155, who will I speak to?
9. If I dial the "unique number" who will I speak to?
10. If I have no cash and no Phonecard, how can I make a phone call from a pay phone?
11. What should I dial after I have dialled 010?
12. If a telephone is flashing "999 calls only", can it be used only for 999 calls?
13. Is it necessary to have a green Phonecard?
14. What is meant by the expression "paid at home"?
15. Which of these services would be most suitable for someone who didn't speak much English and why?

61

SECTION 3

Information on International Calls

When you're in the UK there's always someone back home who would like a call from you. British Telecom has a range of international telephone services to suit your needs.

- WAYS OF CALLING -

Home Direct Operator (no cash required, paid at home)

By dialling a unique number, you can make a Collect or telephone credit card call through an operator back home. This International Cashless Calling service is available from most British Telecom phones in the UK.

UK Operator 155 (no cash required, paid at home)

Simply dial 155, and the UK International Operator will connect you to the number you require. Again, you can choose to call Collect or use your telephone credit card. This International Cashless Calling service is available from most British Telecom phones in the UK.

International Direct Dialling (no operator required, paid in UK)

Simply dial 010 and your own country code, followed by your own area code and local number. With British Telecom's International Direct Dialling you can call over 180 countries from most British Telecom phones in the UK.

- BRITISH TELECOM PAYPHONES -

Payphone (collect/telephone credit card/Coins)

You can usually call Collect or charge to your telephone credit card from a payphone - even if it is flashing "999 calls only". Payphones accept coins to the value of £1, 50p, 20p, 10p, 5p and 2p. You'll need at least £1 to make an International Direct Dialled call. British Telecom payphones are widely available throughout the UK.

Phonecard Payphone (phonecard/collect/telephone credit cards)

This looks similar to a payphone, but only accepts prepaid green Phonecards, which vary in value and are available at Post Offices and shops displaying a green Phonecard sign. However, you can also make Collect or telephone credit card calls from one of these phones, without inserting a green Phonecard.

Short Answers

Stage 3: Write the Answers

Stage 4: Check your Work ☑

Checklist: Short Answers

1. Have you completed the task? ☐
2. Have you answered as briefly as possible? ☐
3. Have you answered all the questions? ☐
4. Have you checked spelling, grammar and punctuation? ☐

SECTION 3

Practice 7

Situation: Your English boss, Sue Pine, is about to visit Grenada for a 10-day business trip. She will be accompanied by her Australian husband and their 7-year old son.

Task: Read the information opposite and answer her questions below. Do not include irrelevant details. Write the answers in your answer book.

(Series 3, 1992, Q2)

Now complete the following stages.

Stage 1: Identify the Task

....

Stage 2: Before you Start

Have you .... ?

Have you .... ?

Questions

1. Is there any disadvantage in using sterling in the local shops?
2. How much airport tax will we have to pay in total when we leave?
3. We want to fly to Caracas afterwards. Which airline(s) connect(s) with Venezuela?
4. When I'm there I want to book a ticket through LIAT. What is the phone number?
5. How many US$ can I take into Grenada?
6. Do I need a passport to enter Grenada?
7. Are there any outlets where credit cards are not generally accepted?
8. Is the main Post Office open on Saturdays?
9. What is the main airport in Grenada and where is it?
10. Is service included in hotel and restaurant bills?
11. Who or what is Grantley Adams?
12. Are the banks open at lunch time?
13. My hotel is in Lance aux Epines; what is the approximate taxi fare from the airport to the hotel?
14. I have to meet someone in Hillsborough. Is this in Grenada?
15. What is the current US$ - EC$ exchange rate?

Short Answers

General Information - Grenada, Carriacou and Petit Martinique are located in the Eastern Caribbean and are the most southerly of the Windward Islands.

International Connections - BWIA flies from Grenada to Aruba, Canada, Caracas, Curacao, Frankfurt, London, New York, Miami (daily), Stockholm and other European cities. LIAT connects with international airlines (British Airways, BWIA, Air Canada, American Airlines, Pan Am, Air France, Lufthansa etc) in Barbados, St Lucia, Trinidad, Martinique and Antigua. BRITISH AIRWAYS flies weekly from London to Grenada.

American Airlines flies daily into Grenada from America through Puerto Rico. ALM flies between Curacao and Grenada - AEROPOSTAL flies between Grenada and Caracas.

Point Salines International Airport is located on the south-west tip of Grenada. There is a Grenada Inter-Line Information desk in the arrival section of the Grantley Adams International Airport in Barbados. The desk is open daily between the hours of 1.00pm to 8.00pm to assist passengers travelling to Grenada.

Caribbean Connections - Apart from the international connections mentioned above, LIAT has daily flights to Carriacou, and other islands in the Caribbean.

Airlines

The following airlines operate on a scheduled basis to Point Salines International Airport.

AEROPOSTAL	444-4732/4736
ALM	440-2796/7
BRITISH AIRWAYS	440-5424/5
BWIA INTERNATIONAL	440-3818/9
LIAT Reservations	440-8788/9
Airport	444-4121/2
Carriacou	443-7362
AMERICAN AIRLINES	444-2222

Public Transport: Buses, mini-buses and taxis.

Taxi Fares: Subject to changes.

Grenada

- The airport to Grand Anse and Lance aux Epines — EC$25.00
- The airport to St. George's — EC$30.00
- Journeys within a one mile radius of the airport — EC$7.00
- Trips outside St. George's
  - first 10 miles (per mile) — EC$4.00
  - thereafter (per mile) — EC$3.00

Carriacou: The airport to Hillsborough — EC$10.00

Customs and Immigration - There is no restriction on the amount of foreign currency which can be brought into Grenada. Clothing and other belongings are also admitted freely, as long as they are for personal use.

British, American and Canadian citizens do not need passports for visits not exceeding three months. An identity document (birth certificate) and a return air ticket are sufficient. For all other nationalities, a valid passport is required. However, any traveller in transit in Trinidad en route to or from Grenada requires a valid passport for their transit stop.

Airport Tax - Departure tax for stays longer than 24 hours is EC$25.00 for adults, EC$12.50 for children aged 10 to 16. Children under 10 are exempt.

Currency - The local currency is the East Caribbean Dollar (EC$) which is pegged to the US$ at a rate of EC$1 to US$.37. It is advisable to exchange your currency or travellers cheques at the banks. Shops and restaurants will accept your own currency but cannot give the most favourable exchange rates.

Credit Cards - Main credit cards are accepted by some hotels but not generally by car rental companies and shops. Travellers cheques are accepted everywhere.

Bank Opening Hours
Monday - Thursday 8.00am to 12.00/2.00pm
Friday - 8.00am to 12.00/1.00pm and 2.30pm to 5.00pm

Banks
Barclays Bank Plc	440-3232
Grenada Bank of Commerce	440-3521

Tipping - A 10% service charge is added by most hotels and restaurants. If no service charge is added, 10% of the bill is suggested as a gratuity.

Electricity - 220/240 Volts 50 cycles, AC. A travel plug is advisable for small appliances.

Shop Opening Hours
Monday to Friday 8.00am - 12 noon and 1.00pm to 4.00pm. Saturday 8.00am - 12.00 noon.

Post Office - The General Post Office in St George's is open Monday to Thursday from 8.00am to 3.30pm and on Fridays until 4.30pm. Sub Post Offices are found in most villages.

SECTION 3

Stage 3: Write the Answers

Stage 4: Check your Work ☑

Checklist: Short Answers

1 Have you completed the task? ☐
2 Have you answered as briefly as possible? ☐
3 Have you answered all the questions? ☐
4 Have you checked spelling, grammar and punctuation? ☐

Short Answers

Practice 8

Situation: You are the Personnel Manager of a fruit juice canning plant in South London and the General Manager, David Hawkins, has asked you for some information about an employee, Carol Winter, in 1992.

Task: Use the information overleaf to answer the following questions briefly but precisely. Do not write on the record form. Write your answers in the answer book.

(Series 2, 1993, Q3)

Now complete the following stages.

Stage 1: Identify the Task

....

Stage 2: Before you Start

Have you .... ?

Have you .... ?

Questions

1. Did she take all of her holiday entitlement in 1992?
2. How many days off did she take for jury service?
3. In which month did she join the firm?
4. In which department is she now?
5. How many days did she work in September?
6. How many days absence did she have in May?
7. How many accidents did she have at work?
8. When did she suffer a death in the family?
9. Was she at work on 14th May?
10. Why wasn't she at work on 4th May?
11. How many days holiday did she take in August?
12. How many days was she absent on business in the first half of the year?
13. How many days was she absent sick in December?
14. How many unexcused absences were there in the whole year?
15. How many times was she absent sick on the day immediately before a bank holiday?
16. How many days was she absent sick in 1992?
17. Was she absent sick in June?
18. Did she have an accident in October?
19. Was she at work on 1st May?
20. On what day was she absent with permission in May?

67

SECTION 3

Name: Carol Winter **Dept:** Technical **Clock No:** 254 **NI No:** FH 273D7
Date of Birth: 19-07-48 **Date of Employment:** 01-02-79 **Sick Days Due:** 5 **Holiday Days Due:** 20

EMPLOYEE ATTENDANCE RECORD

1992	1	2	3	4	5	6	7	8	9	10	11	12	13	14	15	16	17	18	19	20	21	22	23	24	25	26	27	28	29	30	31
JAN	P	S		W	W				W	W						AO	S	W	W	S			W	W			W	W			
FEB	W	W					W	W					W	W	S				W	W							F	W	•	•	
MAR	W				S	W	W	H	H	H	H	W	W										W	W					W	W	
APR		W	W						W	W			A	S	P	W	W	P	S	S			W	W					•		
MAY	W	W	P				W	W			E		W	W						W	W	P	S					W	W		
JUN		S	W	W					W	W					W	W			AO	S	W	W						•			
JUL		W	W				W	W			S	S	W	W					W	W											
AUG	W	W			W	W	H	H	H	H	W	W	H	H	H	H	H	W	W	H	H	H	H	W	W	P					
SEP	X		W	W				W	W		E		W	W			S F	W	W					•							
OCT		W	W				S	W	W			A	E	W	W				S	W	W						W				
NOV	W				W	W					S	W	W			S F	S F	W	W				X	W	W	•					
DEC		W	W				W	W		E		W	W			P	P	W	S F												

Absence Summary	A	AO	D	F	H	J	L	B	S	SF	X	E
JAN		1							2		1	
FEB				1					1			
MAR					5				1			
APR	1								3			
MAY									1			1
JUN		1							2			
JUL									3			
AUG					15							
SEP									1	1	1	
OCT	1								2			1
NOV									1	2	1	
DEC										1		1

A	Accident at Work	H	Holiday	
AO	Accident Elsewhere	J	Jury Duty	
D	Discipline	L	Leave of Absence	
F	Death in Family	B	Absent on Business	
P	Public/Bank Holiday	W	Weekend	
S	Personal Sickness	SF	Sickness in Family	
X	Unexcused Absence	E	Excused Absence	

68

Short Answers

Stage 3: Write the Answers

Stage 4: Check your Work ☑

Checklist: Short Answers

1 Have you completed the task? ☐
2 Have you answered as briefly as possible? ☐
3 Have you answered all the questions? ☐
4 Have you checked spelling, grammar and punctuation? ☐

SECTION 3

Practice 9

Situation: You work in the Training Department of a large chain of supermarkets and you have been asked to prepare answers to questions which will be given to management trainees.

Task: Opposite you will find a page from the index of the supermarket handbook. Using the information on this page state which section and sub section you would consult for advice on the following matters.

Note: *Write your answers in the answer book.*
(Series 1, 1991, Q3)

Now complete the following stages.

Stage 1: Identify the Task

....

Stage 2: Before you Start

Have you .... ?

Have you .... ?

Questions

1. A question from an employee about pension contributions.
2. A worker needs time off to serve on a jury.
3. What to do if something is found in the store.
4. A customer tells the Manager he can smell gas.
5. How long a teenager can work.
6. What to do when prices are to go up.
7. Training new staff.
8. An employee falls and breaks a leg.
9. How to mark the prices of special offers.
10. The Manager is offered a free sample.
11. Fire Prevention Notices.
12. A newspaper reporter asks about price rises.
13. If a customer returns goods.
14. A rat is found in the rubbish area.
15. A training course for the Manager.
16. A complaint that a female employee has been treated unfairly.
17. Who should have to wear overalls.
18. Products which have the wrong label.
19. An employee doing something against the interests of the company.
20. Who is entitled to take maternity leave.

Short Answers

	Section	Sub Section		Section	Sub Section
Gas Leaks - Emergency Procedure	2	3.1	Pallets - Safe Use of	2	2.7
Gifts and Free Samples	2	6.18	Passageways - Safety	2	2.8
Grievance Procedure	3	13	Payroll Procedures	3	18
Status Quo	3	13.2	Payroll Exception Reports	3	18.1
Stages	3	13.3	Completion of	3	18.2
			Forms	3	7.1/7.4 18.3
Health & Safety Policy Statement	1	2.12	Additional Reporting Routines	3	18.5
Health & Safety at Work Act	2	2	Payroll and Payback Control Sheet	3	18.4
Holiday Entitlement - Maternity Leave	3	11.3	Pension Scheme	3	8
Hoists			Benefit	3	8.4
Faults	2	2.2	Cash Option	3	8.5
Insurers Inspection	2	2.3	Contributions	3	8.2
Hose Reels	2	1.4	Death Benefits	3	8.6
Hours of Work - Young Persons	3	3.10/3.12	Joining	3	8.8
Housekeeping - Environmental Health	2	2.8	Life Assurance	3	8.7
			Qualification	3	8.1
Induction Training	3	19.1	Personnel and Training Body	3	1
Inflammable Goods - Fire Risk	2	1.4	Pest Control	2	2.8
In-Store Lettings	1	6.1	Petrol Stations - Fire Instruction	2	1.5
Insurance	2	4	Power Cuts - Emergency Procedures	2	3.2
Cert of Employment Liability	1	2.12	Price		
Insurers Inspection	2	2.3	Decreases	1	2.3
Intoxicating Substances			Error Corrections	1	2.5
(Supply) Act 1985	1	2.10	Increases	1	2.5
			Price Marking		
Job Skills, Training	3	19.1	Price Checking/Off-Paks	1	2.3
Jury Service	3	7.3	Bargain Offers Order 1979	1	2.6
			Correction of Errors	1	2.5
Key Control	2	6.11	Food Order	1	2.4
Key Holders	2	6.10	New Stock	1	2.5
Kiddie Rides	2	6.1	Promotions - Pricing	1	2.5
			Protective Clothing		
Labelling of Goods	1	2.7	Storage of	2	2.8
Life Assurance	3	8.7	Wearing of	2	2.4
Lifting of Merchandise	2	2.6	Public Relations	1	1.9
Lifts					
Failure	2	3.3	Quality of Food Products	1	2.8
Faults, Reporting of	2	2.3/2.7			
Insurers Inspection	2	2.3	Race Relations	3	3.2
Power Failure	2	2.7/3.3	Recognition and Procedural		
Safe Use of	2	2.7	Agreement (USDAW)	3	12
Lockers	2	2.8/6.17		1	2.12
Lost and Found	2	6.15	Recruitment	3	19.1
			Refrigerators - Faulty Doors	2	2.7
Major Injuries - Reporting of	2	2.1	Rehabilitation of Offenders Act	3	3.4
Management Training Scheme (Retail)	3	19.2	Rentals	1	6.1
Maternity Benefit	3	11	Reporting Procedures		
Antenatal Care	3	11.4	Enforcement Officers	1	2.11
Holiday Entitlement	3	11.3	Retail Food & Allied Trades		
Pay	3	11.2	Wages Council	1	2.12
Qualification for	3	11.1	Retail Management Training Scheme	3	19.2
Return to Work	3	11.5	Retail Training Courses	3	19.3
Meat			Return Procedures - Goods	1	3
Unit Pricing of	1	2.4	Robbery	2	6.14
Food Hygiene	2	2.9	Rubbish		
Media Enquiries	1	1.9	Disposal of	2	1.4
Merchandisers	1	6	Fire Risk	2	1.4
Misconduct	3	14.3			
Multiple Food Trade			SAYE Share Option Scheme	3	9
Joint Committee Agreement	1	2.12	Scales - Provision of	1	2.2
			Security	2	6
Notice Boards	2	2.12	Preventative	2	6.9
Notices			Selection - Staff	3	19.1
Health & Safety	2	2.8	Sell by Date	1	2.7
Fire	2	1.4	Service Counters	1	1.5
			Sex Discrimination	3	3.1
Off-Paks	1	2.3	Share Option Scheme	3	9
			Shelves - Safe Stacking of	2	2.5
			Shops Act 1950-65	1	2.12
			Shops Act 1950-65	3	3.9

SECTION 3

Stage 3: Write the Answers

Stage 4: Check your Work ☑

Checklist: Short Answers

1. Have you completed the task? ☐
2. Have you answered as briefly as possible? ☐
3. Have you answered all the questions? ☐
4. Have you checked spelling, grammar and punctuation? ☐

Short Answers

Practice 10

Situation: Your boss is soon to make his first visit to Australasia and has asked you to find the answers to certain questions so that he will be better prepared for his negotiations.

Task: Use the information on the next page, taken from an article on "Doing Business Downunder"* to answer his questions hereunder.

(Series 4, 1991, Q2)

Now complete the following stages.

Stage 1: Identify the Task

....

Stage 2: Before you Start

Have you .... ?

Have you .... ?

Questions

1. How do Australians and New Zealanders feel about each other?
2. Must I wear a jacket at business meetings?
3. What are suitable gifts for my host and hostess if I'm invited to someone's home?
4. Why do the Australians encourage foreign groups to visit?
5. In business, who is more like the English, the Australians or the New Zealanders?
6. How far is New Zealand from Australia by plane?
7. What is the status of women in the business world?
8. Are all the offices air-conditioned?
9. If I am invited to the function by a business associate, who should start talking about business?
10. Are there any problems in giving large, expensive gifts to business associates?
11. Do companies have a policy on their staff receiving gifts?
12. Are business meetings usually easy-going sessions?
13. Does the Australians' directness make them bad negotiators?
14. What is the capital of Australia?
15. How many states and territories are there?

* Downunder = Australia and New Zealand

SECTION 3

General

Australia, like America, is a land of opportunity and the attitude to business is very much a one of "taking the initiative" and seizing the main chance. Thus, an individual's status in the community is based on achievement, rather than birth or education.

As the Australians are very conscious of their geographical isolation, they positively encourage cultural, commercial and political groups to tour their country and see at first hand what all the six states and the two territories (Northern Territory and the Australian Capital Territory (Canberra)), have to offer.

Business Meetings and Dress

Despite the image of "Bondi Beach", business meetings are characterised by their vigorous pace and no nonsense atmosphere. Australians are straightforward and may be considered more direct and possibly louder than their British counterparts. This, however, should not be mistaken for a lack of sophistication - they are very astute negotiators.

Although most offices are air conditioned and the heat is not a problem, it is rarely obligatory to wear a jacket.

Gifts and Socialising

Most Australian companies have a corporate policy on the acceptance of gifts. You should take care when you offer large expensive items as these could be considered a bribe. If you are invited to someone's home, it is, however, perfectly acceptable, indeed polite, to take small gifts for your host and family. (Perhaps whisky for the host, chocolates for the hostess). Entertainment of business associates outside the home is usually very lavish and is not a time for discussing business unless the matter is raised by the host.

Women in Business

Women, especially in the 25-35 year old bracket, have gained a high status in the business world, in particular in the private sector, so do not be surprised to find yourself dealing with a female Manager.

New Zealand

Business methods here tend to be a little more "English" and reserved. There is a slight antipathy between the New Zealanders and the Australians, so do not consider New Zealand as "just another state" of Australia - this could cause offence. The two countries are several hours apart by plane and have noticeably different national characteristics.

Stage 3: Write the Answers

Stage 4: Check your Work ✓

Checklist: Short Answers

1. Have you completed the task? ☐
2. Have you answered as briefly as possible? ☐
3. Have you answered all the questions? ☐
4. Have you checked spelling, grammar and punctuation? ☐

SECTION 3

SECTION 4: True or False

Introduction

The type of question requiring true/false answers may occur in Question 2.

Stage 1: Identify the Task

True or false questions are similar to short answers in that there is often a lot of text or information. Before you start to read this, look at the instructions carefully to see exactly what you have to do. Instructions often say, Write "**True**" or "**False**" and then state your reasons briefly or, Write "**True**" or "**False**" for each statement and give brief details to justify your answer.

Stage 2: How to Complete the Task

When you have read through the task **do not panic** when you see a lot of text. You are only looking to see if the statements are true or false and to give brief details. The best approach is:

1   Read **all** the statements first.
2   Read **all** the text before deciding whether the individual statements are true or false.
3   Read the statements **one at a time** and look for the relevant sentences.

Remember:

- the information in the text is not always in the same order as the statements
- make sure you give the correct details when you justify your answer
- if you don't understand words in the text, try to guess, otherwise ignore them
- if you can't find the correct information, go onto the next statement and come back to it later

Stage 3: How to Answer

You should first of all say whether the statement is "True" or "False." If required, write a short sentence or phrase giving the relevant information from the text. Make sure all your answers are easy to read.

Stage 4: Check Your Work

Checklist: True or False

The following is a list of points to check when you answer true or false.

1   Have you completed the task?
2   Have you answered as briefly as possible?
3   Have you answered all the questions?
4   Have you checked spelling, grammar and punctuation?

SECTION 4

Practice 1

Situation: For an article in a travel magazine you have been asked to check some information about some hotels.

Task: Read the extract from a press release below and say whether the following statements are true or false. Write "**True**" or "**False**" for each statement against the number and give brief details to justify your answer.

(Series 2, 1992, Q2)

Stage 1: Identify the Task
Say whether the statements are true or false.

Stage 2: Before you Start
Have you read through **all** the statements?
Have you read through **all** the information?

Statements

1 EuroHotels Ltd is a competitor of Euraccom plc.
2 Gatwick's *atrium is larger than that of the Heathrow Lake.
3 It is not possible to choose room-service items via the TV system in the hotel rooms.
4 Lake and Dale Hotels are designed to compete with each other.
5 Messages must be collected at Reception by the occupants of the hotel rooms.
6 Schari wanted to invest more money.
7 Squirrel is the catering company used by the hotels.
8 The first Dale hotel will open at Manchester.
9 The Heathrow Lake is larger than the Gatwick Lake.
10 EuroAir passengers can reserve a seat from their hotel room without using the phone.

*recession = fall in business
*piazza = open square
*reluctant = unwilling
*sophisticated = smart and up to date
*atrium = inner courtyard surrounded by building
*monitors = controls, keeps a check on

Airport Hotels for the 1990's

A new hotel group opens a luxurious hotel at Gatwick Airport this month. The name of this new company is EuroHotels Ltd, a wholly-owned subsidiary of Euraccom plc. Set up two years ago, EuroHotels is developing two complementary chains of hotels, Lake and Dale. The first two five-star Lake hotels in Britain will be at Heathrow and Gatwick, with the 500-bedroom Gatwick Lake opening first, followed next month by the 444-bedroom Heathrow Lake at Terminal 4.

The medium-priced Dale chain has already celebrated its UK debut with the 350-bedroom hotel at Manchester. This opened last month and marked a £15 million investment and a new direction for the Euraccom Group at a time when other hotel groups of this kind, notably the Swiss group, Schari, were worrying about the *recession and *reluctant to expand.

The Heathrow and Gatwick Lakes represent an investment of £50 million, investment evident in design which incorporates, in the case of Heathrow, a unique glass-walled, five-storey *atrium, containing the restaurants, bar and lounge areas in a *piazza setting. Gatwick's slightly more modest 32 metre high atrium offers a similar combination of *sophisticated and informal eating areas.

Extensive investment has also gone into providing the very latest computer technology. Squirrel InfoView systems in every room offer, via the TV screen, up-to-the-minute airport, airline and hotel information and room service selection. The TV relays any messages taken for the room occupant, *monitors the room service extra charges and can even take credit card payments on check-out. If you are flying EuroAir you can also check-in your baggage and reserve a seat via the screen.

True or False

Stage 3: Write the Answers

1	False	EuroHotels is a subsidiary of Euraccom plc.
2	False	Gatwick's atrium is more modest.
3	False	It is possible via the TV system.
4	False	Lake Hotels are 5-star and Dale Hotels are medium-priced.
5	False	The TV relays any messages to the rooms.
6	False	Schari were reluctant to invest money.
7	False	Squirrel is the TV InfoView system.
8	False	The Dale Hotel has already opened in Manchester.
9	False	Heathrow has 444 beds and Gatwick 500.
10	True	EuroAir passengers can reserve a seat via the TV.

Stage 4: Check your Work ✓

Checklist: True or False

1. Have you completed the task? ✓
2. Have you answered as briefly as possible? ✓
3. Have you answered all the questions? ✓
4. Have you checked spelling, grammar and punctuation? ✓

79

SECTION 4

Practice 2

Situation: You are required to write an article for a trade magazine about developments in the drinks industry.

Task: In order to clarify your mind before writing, read the article below and say whether the statements below are "**True**" or "**False**". Give brief details to justify your answer. Do **not** write on the question paper. Write only your answers in the answer book.

(Series 1, 1993, Q2)

Stage 1: Identify the Task
Say whether the statements are true or false.

Stage 2: Before you Start
Have you read through **all** the statements?
Have you read through **all** the information?

Statements

1. FAE is the sales department of Carstensen Brothers.
2. Fewer then 500 people work at the Birmingham branch.
3. The Lee Green plant has not grown before this year.
4. The move to Lee Green will cause job losses in London.
5. The growth in production will not cost any extra money.
6. The Birmingham branch was the first to introduce fruit juice drinks in ready-to-serve containers.
7. Gerry Hitchens is the International Marketing Manager of CB.
8. CB produces alcoholic drinks.
9. The Birmingham factory was not the main plant.
10. A new bottling plant is already working at Lee Green.

Carstensen Brothers is closing its Birmingham drinks factory in May this year and switching production to Lee Green in South East London. The company plans to expand the production of bottled and canned health-orientated beverages at the 65 acre site.

In the last 5 years Carstensen Bros has invested more than £10 million to modernise and expand the Lee Green factory. The latest investment - a new £9 million bottling operation - went into production last year.

"We now plan to spend £4.75 million to increase capacity and output at Lee Green, which will increase our competitive edge," said Gerry Hitchens, UK Chairman of CB Consumer Brands, at a press conference this week at the company headquarters at Vaughan-Rees Tower in Lee Green.

About 90 new job opportunities will be created and first consideration will be given to any of the 600 staff at the Birmingham branch who wish to move.

The CB unit at Lee Green was claimed as the UK leader in pioneering the introduction of fruit juice drinks in ready-to-serve cartons. Ready-to-drink Rejuv, according to the company, remains the brand leader in this section and this year Lee Green will produce 290 million packs.

According to market researchers FAE, the ready-to-drink health-orientated drinks market is worth some £5.5 billion per annum.

True or False

Stage 3: Write the Answers

1	False	FAE are market researchers.
2	False	600 staff work at the Birmingham branch.
3	False	£10 million has been invested over the last 5 years to expand the Lee Green Plant.
4	False	About 90 new job opportunities will be created.
5	False	The growth in production will cost £4.75 million.
6	False	The CB unit at Lee Green was the first.
7	False	Gerry Hitchens is the UK Chairman of CB Consumer Brands.
8	False	CB produces health-orientated drinks.
9	True	The company headquarters is at Lee Green.
10	True	It went into operation last year.

Now complete the following stage.

Stage 4: Check your Work ☑

Checklist: True or False
1. Have you completed the task? ☐
2. Have you answered as briefly as possible? ☐
3. Have you answered all the questions? ☐
4. Have you checked spelling, grammar and punctuation? ☐

SECTION 4

Practice 3

Situation: Below you will find an extract from a tapescript of Dr Standen talking about his work in a pharmaceutical company.

Task: Read the extract below and say whether the statements are "**True**" or "**False**". Give brief answers to justify your choice.

"....then as far as the structure is concerned, we have a Medical Director, Dr Horton, who obviously looks after the whole department, but spends most of his time at policy meetings. He has a lot of outside responsibilities too. Since March his deputy, as Director of Medical Research, has been Dr Graveney, who joined us from Glucon plc. He's taken a lot of the workload from Dr Horton for the Clinical Research Department.

There are two clinical research managers: Peter Coldwell does Phase 3 work and I do Phase 4. He works for Germany and I work for the UK operation. We also have a Medical Adviser, Jim Flavell, who is responsible for Phase 2. Going down a level, Andy Kenyon and Dr. Richardson work for me as clinical research associates. Coldwell's assistants are Paul Booth, who is seconded from ICI and Mr Headley, who is at the moment working on Lisab, our new pain-killer. In the field, ultimately responsible to the Medical Adviser, there are 64 research officers who report in the first instance to the regional manager."

(Series 4, 1989, adapted version)

Stage 1: Identify the Task
Say whether the statements are true or false.

Stage 2: Before you Start
Have you read through **all** the statements?
Have you read through **all** the information?

Statements

1. The extract is taken from a book by Dr Standen.
2. Andy Kenyon is Dr Richardson's clinical research associate.
3. Peter Coldwell does Phase 3 and Phase 4 work.
4. Peter Coldwell is Paul Booth's assistant.
5. Dr Graveney used to work for Glucon plc.
6. Dr Standen works for Germany.
7. Lisab is ICI's new pain-killer.
8. 64 research officers are responsible to Jim Flavell.
9. Dr Horton is deputy Medical Director.
10. Mr Headley works for ICI.

True or False

Now complete the following stages.

Stage 3: Write the Answers

Stage 4: Check your Work ☑

Checklist: True or False

1. Have you completed the task? ☐
2. Have you answered as briefly as possible? ☐
3. Have you answered all the questions? ☐
4. Have you checked spelling, grammar and punctuation? ☐

SECTION 4

Practice 4

Situation: A colleague is giving a talk about the Channel Tunnel to a group of students and has asked you to check some information.

Task: Read the information opposite and state whether the following statements are "**True**" or "**False**". Quote **briefly** from the text to justify each answer. Do **not** write on the question paper; write your answers in the answer book.

(Series 4, 1992, Q2)

Stage 1: Identify the Task

Say whether the statements are true or false.

Now complete the following stages.

Stage 2: Before you Start

Have you .... ?

Have you .... ?

Statements

1   Some 6,000 people are likely to be made redundant when the Tunnel is completed.

2   Some Britons might live in Northern France yet continue to work in London.

3   The Channel Tunnel will connect Dover with Boulogne.

4   John Major was the Prime Minister who finally agreed that the project should go ahead.

5   The smallest tunnel is for passengers.

6   There are more French workers than British workers employed on the construction of the Tunnel.

7   The Tunnel will open on time.

8   The South coast of England will gain more from the project than London.

9   It is thought that the property market in Northern France will suffer a decline.

10   The Tunnel is becoming more expensive to build as time passes.

True or False

The Channel Tunnel

The Eurotunnel project was ratified on 29th July 1987 by both the English Prime Minister, at that time Margaret Thatcher, and President Francois Mitterand.

The work for the Channel Tunnel consists in the building of three tunnels between Castle Hill Portal, near Folkestone, and Beussingue Portal, near Calais.

A hundred metres under the sea the tunnels will be some 50km long. The two tunnels for rail traffic are seven point six metres in diameter. A third tunnel, four point eight metres in diameter, is especially designed for maintenance, as well as for emergency access.

In order to carry out this work, six thousand five hundred British people and three thousand five hundred French people are employed. Six drill machines are also working on the sites.

Many consequences for the economies of both countries are expected from this work. From the British point of view, once the Tunnel is finished, most of the sea transport will disappear and about six thousand people working in the harbours and on the ferries will lose their jobs.

In fact, the Tunnel will be much more profitable for the British capital than for the local region. The long-term forecasts see the Tunnel as the best way to attract businessmen to the City of London.

From the French point of view, in addition to the job creation during the construction, the hopes are for the extension of tourism in the North of France, as well as a boom in local property sales as wealthy Britons consider buying a holiday home there or even commuting from there to work in London.

The estimated cost of the Tunnel is £20 billion, but it could even reach £35 billion as the Tunnel suffers not only from extra cost but also from delay in the delivery of trains especially built for rail traffic under sea.

For these reasons, among others, the opening of this link between England and France will not be on the 15th June 1993, as previously planned, but during the winter of 1993.

SECTION 4

Stage 3:   Write the Answers

                        Stage 4:   Check your Work ☑
                        Checklist: True or False
                        1   Have you completed the task?   ☐
                        2   Have you answered as briefly as possible?   ☐
                        3   Have you answered all the questions?   ☐
                        4   Have you checked spelling, grammar and punctuation?   ☐

True or False

Practice 5

Situation: A recent government survey gave figures for the number of smokers in the working population of Britain. The survey compared the situation in 1968 with that in 1988.

Task: Analyse the government figures in the following table. Then complete the statements that follow.

Note: *Write your answers in your answer booklet. Do not write on this question paper.*
(Series 2, 1989, Q3)

	1968		1988	
AGE	MALE	FEMALE	MALE	FEMALE
20-30	50%	25%	40%	40%
30-40	60%	30%	25%	30%
40-50	70%	35%	40%	25%
50-60	70%	35%	50%	25%
OVERALL	63%	32%	43%	32%
Male & Female	48%		34%	

Smoking among the British workforce
1968 - 1988

Now complete the following stages.

Stage 1: Identify the Task

....

Stage 2: Before you Start

Have you .... ?

Have you .... ?

SECTION 4

A Complete statements 1-5 with a **fraction** (eg a third, a quarter, a half, etc).

1 In 1968 a little less than .... of the British workforce smoked.

2 In 1988 a little more than .... of the British workforce smoked.

3 In 1968 nearly .... of the men smoked.

4 In 1968 nearly .... of the women smoked.

5 In 1988 less than .... of the men smoked and less

   than .... of the women smoked.

B Compare the following groups of people. State whether the first group smoked **more**, **less** or the **same** amount as the second group.

6 Males in 1968 compared with males in 1988.

7 Females in 1968 compared with females in 1988.

8 Males aged 20-30 in 1968 compared with males aged 20-30 in 1988.

9 Females aged 20-30 in 1968 compared with females aged 20-30 in 1988.

10 Males aged 30-40 in 1968 compared with males aged 30-40 in 1988.

11 Females aged 30-40 in 1968 compared with females aged 30-40 in 1988.

12 Males aged 20-30 in 1988 compared with females aged 20-30 in 1988.

13 Males aged 20-30 in 1968 compared with males aged 30-40 in 1968.

14 Males aged 20-30 in 1988 compared with males aged 30-40 in 1988.

15 The total workforce in 1968 compared with the total workforce in 1988.

C State whether each of these statements is **true** or **false**. Also, briefly **give information from the table** to show why each sentence is true or false.

16 Smoking among the British workforce decreased between 1968 and 1988.

17 Smoking among working males decreased between 1968 and 1988.

18 Smoking among working females decreased between 1968 and 1988.

19 Smoking among young women decreased between 1968 and 1988.

20 Quite a lot of females who were aged 30-40 in 1968 had given up smoking by 1988.

True or False

Stage 3: Write the Answers

Stage 4: Check your Work ☑
Checklist: True or False

1 Have you completed the task? ☐
2 Have you answered as briefly as possible? ☐
3 Have you answered all the questions? ☐
4 Have you checked spelling, grammar and punctuation? ☐

89

SECTION 4

Practice 6

Situation: Your department has asked you to check some facts regarding the acceptance of credit cards in supermarkets.

Task: Read the extract from a newspaper article opposite and say whether the following statements are "**True**" or "**False**". Write "True" or "False" for each statement and give brief details to justify your answer, which should bear the number of the statement it refers to.

(Series 1, 1992, Q2)

Now complete the following stages.

Stage 1: Identify the Task

....

Stage 2: Before you Start

Have you .... ?

Have you .... ?

Statements

1 Buyz and Ecognom have accepted credit cards for over 10 years.

2 Fewer than 10% of Tristans' customers use direct debit cards.

3 Credit cards are not popular with people who buy large quantities.

4 It appears that consumers are becoming more careless in their use of credit cards.

5 The Accrington and Swindon branches will accept credit cards from next week.

6 Tristans have accepted credit cards in 20 outlets.

7 Tristans are paying more that other companies to the credit card companies.

8 Tristans is the first supermarket chain to accept credit cards.

9 Tristans' good experience with direct debit cards has persuaded the chain to accept credit cards.

10 Tristans think that accepting credit cards will attract new customers.

True or False

The supermarket chain, Tristans, is to accept credit cards in its supermarkets after deciding its objections to them are "no longer valid".

The £8.2 billion food giant is to put Visa, Access, Mastercard and Martincard on trial in 12 of its outlets. The process started in Lee Green last week, with Accrington, Kinver, Wollaston, Swindon, Brierly and Quarry to follow next month.

Tristans say that a number of changes have been made to credit card usage which has made their introduction more acceptable. It is understood that the chain has negotiated a reduction in the fee that it has to pay to the credit card companies.

In addition, there has been a reduction in the number of credit card users and the introduction of an annual fee, both of which have convinced Tristans that the customers are using the cards more responsibly.

Tristans say: "We see this as an extension of choice and bringing in new customers, especially those who prefer this method of payment when purchasing in bulk."

Tristans say that their experience with direct debit cards* has prompted it to accept credit cards. "We would never have tested credit cards if it had not been for debit cards," said James Kirk, Financial Director of the company.

The supermarket chain claims that it accounts for over 30% of the direct debit market. More than ten per cent of its customers use this means of payment, accounting for more than 27% of trade.

Up to now, Tristans has lagged behind its rivals in accepting credit cards. Buyz and Ecognom have done so since 1988.

---

* Direct debit cards = plastic cards issued by banks etc to account holders which allow money to be deducted directly from the account to pay for the goods purchased.

SECTION 4

Stage 3:   Write the Answers

Stage 4:   Check your Work ☑

Checklist: True or False

1. Have you completed the task? ☐
2. Have you answered as briefly as possible? ☐
3. Have you answered all the questions? ☐
4. Have you checked spelling, grammar and punctuation? ☐

True or False

Practice 7

Situation: For an article in a local newspaper you have been asked to check some details of a local company's Fire Safety Procedures.

Task: On the next page you will find an extract from the Fire Safety Procedures of a supermarket. Use this information to say whether the following statements are "**True**" or "**False**". State "**True**" or "**False**" and give brief details to justify your answers.

(Series 3, 1991, Q2)

Now complete the following stages.

Stage 1: Identify the task

....

Stage 2: Before you Start

Have you .... ?

Have you .... ?

Statements

1. Any member of staff can test the automatic fire alarm.
2. Every fire alarm should be tested weekly.
3. Every member of staff must be trained to use a fire extinguisher.
4. Fire extinguishers can be used to keep fire doors open.
5. Only certain members of staff need to know how to turn off the electricity at the mains.
6. The fire extinguishers are to be checked more often than the sprinklers.
7. The hoses must be checked every time a fire drill takes place.
8. The manager must inspect the fire certificate every two months.
9. The maximum width of the gangways is 1 metre.
10. Things that burn easily should not be piled up near fluorescent lights.

SECTION 4

Fire Safety Procedures

Fire Drills
To be conducted every six months. All staff must be taken around the store to ensure that they know every fire exit, means of escape and what to do in an emergency, including how to use fire extinguishers.

Fire Extinguishers
To be checked weekly for defects, contents, pressure reading and correct location.
Fire extinguishers must not be moved from specified location or used as door stops.

Sprinklers
To be tested weekly.

Fire Alarms
One fire alarm call point to be tested each week. All call points to be numbered sequentially and tested in numerical order. Where stores have automatic alarms, the telephone line must be tested daily by the manager or his/her deputy.

Hose Reels
To be tested once every six months in conjunction with the fire drill.

Gangways
Gangways must be kept clear at all times and must never be less than 1 metre in width. White lined areas must not be used for storage of goods or equipment.

Exits
Must be kept clear of obstruction at all times. Exit doors are not to be locked during working hours. Fire Exit doors must never be jammed open.

Fire Check Doors
Fire check doors must never be jammed open. Must be tested once every 13 weeks to ensure closing mechanism is operational.

Fire Notices
All notices relating to fire prevention and instructions must be checked weekly.

Fire Certificate
The fire certificate must be kept in a safe place in the manager's office readily available for inspection by the Fire Brigade.

Electricity/Gas Intakes
All members of the fire fighting party must know the exact location of the electricity mains power intake switch, and the gas metre turncock.

Rubbish/Inflammable Goods
Rubbish and cardboard waste must be kept to a minimum. External storage areas should be kept tidy, preferably away from buildings and equipment. Highly inflammable material must not be stacked in or near letter boxes, fluorescent lighting or motor rooms.

Stage 3: Write the Answers

Stage 4: Check your Work ☑

Checklist: True or False

1. Have you completed the task? ☐
2. Have you answered as briefly as possible? ☐
3. Have you answered all the questions? ☐
4. Have you checked spelling, grammar and punctuation? ☐

SECTION 4

Practice 8

Situation: Your company is going to re-locate to Docklands in London. At a recent staff meeting several members of staff asked you about how they could reach the new premises by public transport. In particular, they wanted to know about the new Docklands Light Railway.

Task: Using the information in the leaflet that you have obtained, say whether the following statements are "**True**" or "**False**". State "**True**" or "**False**" and give brief details to justify your answer.

(Series 2, 1990, Q2 adapted)

Now complete the following stages.

Stage 1: Identify the Task

....

Stage 2: Before you Start

Have you .... ?

Have you .... ?

Statements

1 Docklands Light Railway has always been popular.

2 Train destinations are only flashed on an Electronic Indicator on station platforms.

3 Train Captains sell tickets to passengers.

4 Lifts are provided for wheelchairs.

5 Alarm buttons are only provided on trains.

6 Engineering work is only carried out at weekends.

7 Coin-operated ticket machines are provided on the platforms.

8 Passengers without tickets may have to pay double the value of the fare avoided.

9 DLR tickets are only valid on the Underground.

10 Group and special tickets cannot be bought on the day.

LEAFLET   **The Docklands Light Railway**

The Docklands Light Railway (DLR) came into being when re-development in Docklands made it essential to improve public transport - both for commuters and local residents. From the start it proved popular and already needs to expand to meet an increasing demand.

All stations are monitored by closed circuit TV. In addition, mobile staff patrol the stations, which are clean and brightly lit. The destination of trains is flashed on an Electronic Indicator on station platforms, and also announced on the public address system.

Every train has a Train Captain, who checks tickets and can answer queries whilst ensuring the smooth operation of the train. All stations have special lifts that take wheelchairs and space is allocated for wheelchairs on the trains. Trains were built to take wheelchairs easily.

Each station is equipped with a passenger alarm (emergency use only) which, when activated by a push button, establishes immediate contact with our control room. There are emergency buttons on trains for passenger use if warranted.

Whilst engineering work is in progress to improve and extend the railway (after 9.30pm and at weekends, until further notice) a special DLR substitute bus service is operated. The railway is controlled from the Operations and Maintenance Centre adjacent to Poplar Station. Queries about the railway are also handled from here (telephone 071-583 0311) or from our 24-hour information service 071-222 1234.

Single journey tickets to all DLR and Underground stations can be bought on the day from the coin-operated ticket machines in station entrance halls. You must have a valid ticket before you travel. Any passenger without a ticket will be dealt with in accordance with the regulations. This may involve payment of an additional fare 10 times the value of the fare avoided, or may lead to prosecution. London Regional Transport and British Rail Travelcards and Capitalcards are valid on DLR trains and substitute buses provided they cover the right fare zones.

DLR tickets are valid on the Underground and British Railways. Group and special tickets can be bought in advance by writing to the Docklands Light Railway, PO Box 154, London E14 9QA, and on the day from the DLR Information Centres at Island Gardens Station (open 10am to 4pm weekdays) or at Tower Gateway Station (open 10.45am to 3.15pm most days).

SECTION 4

Stage 3:   Write the Answers

Stage 4:   Check your Work ☑

Checklist: True or False

1. Have you completed the task? ☐
2. Have you answered as briefly as possible? ☐
3. Have you answered all the questions? ☐
4. Have you checked spelling, grammar and punctuation? ☐

True or False

Practice 9

Situation: Your company is considering issuing British Telecom (BT) Chargecards to some executives.

Task: Study the text on the next page and say whether the following statements are "**True**" or "**False**". Give brief details from the extract to justify your answers. Do not write on your question paper. Write the answers in your answer book.

(Series 3, 1993, Q2)

Now complete the following stages.

Stage 1: Identify the Task

....

Stage 2: Before you Start

Have you .... ?

Have you .... ?

Statements

1. A request form for a chargecard is on the other side of the information sheet.

2. It is possible to use the chargecard to call the UK from over 100 countries.

3. Chargecards cannot be used to make fax transmissions.

4. Quickcalls mean that you can dial the whole number quickly.

5. The maximum daily allowance on a chargecard is £199.

6. There are fewer than 25,000,000 phones in the UK.

7. Using a chargecard is more expensive than using a BT public payphone.

8. Value Added Tax is not recoverable on calls from public payphones by chargecard.

9. You pay a fee for each chargecard.

10. Your phone bill does not show details of every call made with a chargecard.

SECTION 4

10 Ways your company will benefit from a BT Chargecard

A BT Chargecard is invaluable for anyone in business. It gives your colleagues the freedom to keep in touch whenever they're out of the office, from over 30 million phones in the UK. And it gives you better financial control of your phone bills through individual call allowances and itemised statements. Here are just a handful of ways your business can benefit from a BT Chargecard.

1   You don't need cash to make a call.

The beauty of a BT Chargecard is that you can make calls from any BT public payphone without the bother of hunting for change. And dialling direct with a BT chargecard costs the same as calling from a BT public payphone.

2   You get more financial control.

You can set a direct-dialled daily allowance on each BT Chargecard your company uses, between £1 - £99 a day. Even if you exceed your allowance, you'll never be cut off in the middle of a call - you'll always be allowed to finish.

3   You needn't rely on your clients generosity.

Because your calls can be charged to your company phone bill, you can always feel at ease when asking to use a client's phone.

4   You can go about your business faster.

Dialling direct with your BT Chargecard can save you time and money. You can also use your BT Chargecard to quickly redial engaged numbers, and to make "Quickcalls" to a number of your choice without the bother of having to dial the whole number.

5   You'll find your finances are easier.

Each BT Chargecard call is itemised on a statement, showing you the date, time, length, cost and number called. So you can easily separate business and personal calls, simplifying your finances.

6   You can use your BT Chargecard for more than just phone calls.

With a BT Chargecard in your pocket you can also use fax machines, pagers and make modem calls, without having to pay at the time of use.

7   You can use over 30 million UK phones.

Wherever business leads you, you can keep in touch with your office from almost any UK phone and charge the cost of your call to your company phone bill.

8   You can reclaim VAT on calls made via BT public payphones.

Using a BT Chargecard can help keep your expenses down. That's because you can reclaim the VAT made on BT Chargecard calls made from BT public payphones.

9   You can tailor your BT Chargecard to suit your needs.

You can choose a full service BT Chargecard which allows you to call to almost anywhere in the world. Plus you can call back to the UK from 120 countries overseas.

10 The BT Chargecard is FREE.

You can request any number of BT Chargecards for your business and it won't cost you anything. You only pay for the calls that are made.

All you need to do is complete the request form overleaf and post it to us free, today.

True or False

Stage 3: Write the Answers

Stage 4: Check your Work ✓

Checklist: True or False

1 Have you completed the task? ☐
2 Have you answered as briefly as possible? ☐
3 Have you answered all the questions? ☐
4 Have you checked spelling, grammar and punctuation? ☐

101

SECTION 4

Practice 10

Situation: For an article in your staff magazine you have been asked to check some information on two companies which are considered good to work for.

Task: Opposite there are two extracts from an article on the companies in London. Use this information to say whether the following statements are true or false. Also, give brief details from the extracts to justify your answers.

Note: **Write your answers in your book**. Write **"True"** or **"False"** and then state your reasons briefly.

(Series 2, 1991, Q2)

Now complete the following stages.

Stage 1: Identify the Task

....

Stage 2: Before you Start

Have you .... ?

Have you .... ?

Statements

1. Account executive is the highest position in the advertising agency.

2. All advertising agency employees must start work at the same time.

3. Crowe, Dugdale and Deakin have an account with Lloyds Bank.

4. Squirrel employees pay the full price for their meals at work.

5. Squirrel employees can use the squash club at the local gym free of charge.

6. Squirrel UK pays secretaries no more than £10,000 per annum.

7. Staff at the advertising agency get more holidays than staff in the computer company.

8. The computer company made more profit than the advertising agency last year.

9. Everyone has a company car at the advertising agency.

10. There are more men than women working for Squirrel.

SQUIRREL COMPUTER UK

Profile
Subsidiary of Squirrel Computer, Minnesota. Launched in 1980.

Company Figures
£2.3 million pre-tax profit last year.

Number of Employees
300.

Employee Turnover
Average four to five years. Ten employees have been there for more than seven years.

Pay
£10,000 minimum for secretaries. £25,000 to £35,000 for managers. Salesmen reaching targets 100% get around £150,000.

Prospects
Internal candidates are given preference wherever possible. 45% of the staff are women.

Holidays
35 days per year. Four week sabbatical on full pay after six years.

Environment
Air-conditioned offices in Central London.

Amenities
Staff squash club and swimming pool on premises. Subsidised canteen.

Dress Code
None.

Perks
Each employee has own personal computer and printer for home use. Health insurance for everyone. Profit-sharing scheme for managerial staff.

Atmosphere
American-style high pressure management. American-style informality: all staff use first names, all staff use same canteen.

CROWE, DUGDALE DEAKIN & PARTNERS

Profile
Independent advertising agency. Formed 1983. Big accounts include Lloyds Bank, Parsifal Lager and Aeroflot.

Company Figures
£2.1 million pre-tax profit last year.

Number of Employees
200.

Employee Turnover
Average stay five years.

Pay
Graduate trainees start at £12,000. Account Executives get £40,000 plus.

Prospects
Several secretaries have become Account Executives. All except three of the Account Directors started as graduate trainees.

Holidays
Four weeks.

Environment
High-class offices in Mayfair.

Amenities
Gymnasium in office basement. Subsidised restaurant.

Dress code
Informal, but "executives are expected to dress appropriately when meeting clients."

Perks
Account Executives and upwards have a company car. Free life and health insurance for everyone.

Atmosphere
Relaxed. Open management style. An unofficial flexitime system operates.

SECTION 4

Stage 3:   Write the Answers

Stage 4:   Check your Work ☑

Checklist: True or False

1   Have you completed the task? ☐
2   Have you answered as briefly as possible? ☐
3   Have you answered all the questions? ☐
4   Have you checked spelling, grammar and punctuation? ☐

SECTION 5: Gap-Fills

Introduction

The type of question requiring you to fill in gaps in text may occur in Question 3.

Stage 1: Identify the Task

This type of question normally has a short piece of text (with gaps in it), based on some other form of information. This may be graphs, charts, tables, etc. Before you start looking at the text and information, read the instructions. These normally read "Write your answer for each numbered space" or "Write your answer in your answer book."

Stage 2: How to Complete the Task

You have to use the information and find a suitable word or number for the gap. The best approach is:

1. Look at the information first (not the text) and work out what it is about, eg
    - what the figures represent
    - what the abbreviations mean
    - what the graphs, charts, tables, etc show
    - Until you understand the information do not go on

2. The next thing to do is to read through all of the gap-fill text. Ignore the gaps. This way you will know what all of the text is about. It will be easier to find suitable words if you know what information comes after this.

3. Go back to the start of the gap-fill exercise and try to find a suitable word or number for each gap. Remember:
    - it is normally one word or number per gap
    - if you cannot find a suitable word, leave it and come back to it later

Stage 3: How to Answer

You should not write the complete text in your book, you should only write the question number with the missing word/number next to it. Make sure all your answers are clearly numbered and are easy to read.

Stage 4: Check your Work

Checklist: Gap-Fills

The following is a list of points to check when you fill in the gaps.

1. Have you completed the task?
2. Have you clearly numbered your answers?
3. Have you found words/numbers for all the gaps?
4. Have you checked spelling, grammar and punctuation?

SECTION 5

Practice 1

Situation: The Napier Automobile Company had three models in production in the 1980's: the Blenheim GLX, a five-seater executive car, the Gladiator GTi, a high-performance four-seater and the Sprite MG, a two-seater sports car. The graph below shows the sales figures for each model from 1980 to 1990.

Task: Using the information in the graph, complete the following account of the production and sales of Napier cars during the 1980's. For each space write a word, a date, or a number as appropriate.

Note: Copy the numbers 1 to 20 from the passage as a list down the page in your answer booklet and then write your answer for each numbered space.

(Series 2, 1990, Q3)

Stage 1: Identify the Task
Write the answer for each numbered space.

Stage 2: Before you Start
Have you read through **all** the information?
Have you looked at the graph?

The Blenheim was already in production in (1).............................. and by 1983 was selling (2).............................per year. At that time it sold (3)..............................than any other model. However, in 1984 sales declined to (4).............................. but they later (5)..............................to 40,000 in (6).............................. Since then sales have remained steady and there has been a slight (7).............................. in recent years. Although sales of the Blenheim were low in 1984, the company's other two models, the Gladiator and the Sprite, both achieved their (8).............................. sales figures in this year. The Gladiator came on to the market in (9).............................. and within (10).............................. years had achieved sales of 55,000 per annum. Sales soon began to decline and by 1988 had reached (11).............................. a year. This model is still in production and sells about (12).............................. per annum. The Napier Auto Company's third model, the Sprite, was in production between (13)..............................and (14).............................. and achieved its highest sales figures in (15).............................. when (16).............................. were sold. Sales declined rapidly however, although they picked up in (17).............................., two years before production of this model (18).............................. . At the end of the decade Napier Autos had (19).............................. cars in production, of which the (20).............................. has been the most successful overall.

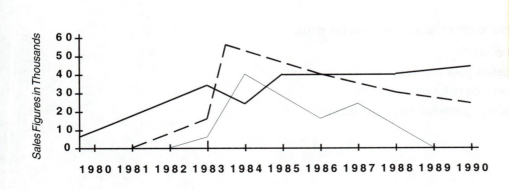

106

Stage 3: Write the Answers

1	1980		11	30,000
2	35,000		12	25,000
3	more		13	1982
4	25,000		14	1989
5	increased		15	1984
6	1985		16	40,000
7	increase		17	1987
8	highest		18	ceased
9	1981		19	2
10	2.5		20	Blenheim

Stage 4: Check your Work ☑

Checklist: Gap-Fills

1. Have you completed the task? ☑
2. Have you clearly numbered your answers? ☑
3. Have you found words for all the gaps? ☑
4. Have you checked spelling, grammar and punctuation? ☑

SECTION 5

Practice 2

Situation: Below you will see a chart showing the merits of various items in a snack bar. Analyse this chart and complete the sentences below.

Task: Write the answers in your answer book.

(Series 2, 1991, Q3)

Stage 1: Identify the Task
Write the answer for each numbered space.

Stage 2: Before you Start
Have you read through **all** the information?
Have you looked at the table?

1. In terms of profitability there were ...... *5* ...... items with a high rating.
2. As far as ease of selling was concerned ...... *sandwiches* ...... stood out as being the best.
3. Because of the method of selling, for both ...... *hot chocolate* ...... (a) .... and ...... *fruit juice* ...... (b) .... wastage was zero.
4. ...... *Ice Cream* ......, like the fruit juice has its own dispenser. So ease of preparation is not a significant factor.
5. The worst item for storage was ...... *salads* ...... (a) ...., which also came bottom for ease of .... (b) ...... *preparation* ......
6. As milk shakes are made to .... (a) ...., there is no entry for the .... (b) .... category.
7. Neither ...... *salad* ...... (a) .... nor ...... *hot chocolate* ...... (b) .... are rated highly for profitability.
8. Both ...... *salads* ...... (a) .... and ...... *milk shakes* ...... (b) .... were poor in terms of ease of ...... *selling* ...... (c) ....
9. According to the footnote*, the .... (a) .... of .... (b) .... did not refer to different types of bread, merely the ...... *fillings* ...... (c) ....
10. There are so many ...... *varieties* ...... (a) .... of ice cream that an extra category of .... (b) .... was allowed, although not mentioned in the ...... *key* ...... (c) ....

	Ease of Preparation	Ease of Storage	Ease of Selling	Profitability	Varieties	Wastage
Sandwiches	G	G	VG	H	H*	L
Salads	VP	VP	P	L	L	H
Soup	G	VG	G	H	H	L
Ice Cream	-	VG	G	H	VH	L
Milk Shakes	P	-	P	H	M	L
Hot Chocolate	G	VG	G	L	-	O
Fruit Juice	-	G	G	H	L	O

Key: VG = Very Good   H = High   G = Good   M = Medium   P = Poor   L = Low   VP = Very Poor

*refers to fillings only

Gap-Fills

Stage 3: Write the Answers

1. five

2. sandwiches

3. (a) hot chocolate
   (b) fruit juice

4. ice cream

5. (a) salads
   (b) preparation

6. (a) order
   (b) ease of storage

7. (a) salads
   (b) hot chocolate

8. (a) milk shakes
   (b) salads
   (c) selling

9. (a) varieties
   (b) sandwiches
   (c) fillings

10. (a) varieties
    (b) very high
    (c) key

Now complete the following stage.

Stage 4: Check your Work ☑

Checklist: Gap-Fills

1. Have you completed the task? ☐
2. Have you clearly numbered your answers? ☐
3. Have you found words for all the gaps? ☐
4. Have you checked spelling, grammar and punctuation? ☐

SECTION 5

Practice 3

Below you will find a diagram of an exhibition hall and an extract from the exhibition organiser's instructions.

Do not write on the diagram. Write the figures in brackets from (1) to (20) in your answer book. Follow the diagram and complete the instructions.
(Series 4, 1991, Q4)

Stage 1: Identify the Task
Write the answer for each numbered space.

Stage 2: Before you Start
Have you read through **all** the information?
Have you looked at the chart?

"... when you come in through the (1).............................entrance on the (2).............................floor, there are (3).............................stands on the left and ten on the right. For your convenience you can see that I've allotted the letters (4).............................to (5).............................for the sections, and numbered the individual (6).............................in the sections. As this floor is for (7).............................interest, to grab the visitor's attention immediately, I suggest that we give Jameson and Co the four small stands in E, immediately on the (8).............................as one enters. The largest stand on this floor, (9).............................we have given to Daniels and Co. The (10).............................stands on the left (section B) just before the stairs we'll give to the games' manufacturers.

Now, on to the exhibitors, who have got the (11).............................floor. Since they are the sponsors, I've given (12).............................the central position, which is (13).............................stands. The other stands I've numbered, starting with those around the (14).............................area. Excluding the central area that makes (15).............................in all on this floor. I've put the local college in the (16).............................stands in the General Education area.

The stairs on the right, ie, next to stand (17).............................lead up to the bar, and on the other side those next to stand (18).............................go to the restaurant. The stairs at the (19).............................end are to the exit from which there is a shuttle service to the (20)............................."

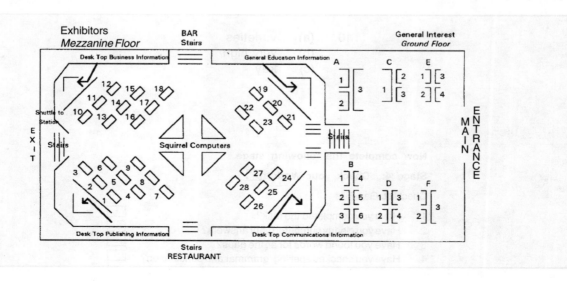

110

Now complete the following stages.

Stage 3: Write the Answers

Gap-Fills

Stage 4: Check your Work ☑

Checklist: Gap-Fills

1. Have you completed the task? ☐
2. Have you clearly numbered your answers? ☐
3. Have you found words for all the gaps? ☐
4. Have you checked spelling, grammar and punctuation? ☐

111

SECTION 5

Practice 4

Situation: You have to keep a record of the monthly expenses claims submitted by sales representatives in your company. To help you do this, you have arranged the figures in a table which indicates in £'s the amount claimed by each representative in each month.

Task: Look at the information in the table and fill in the spaces in the following report, using a word or number for each space.

Note: Copy the numbers 1 to 20 from the passage as a list down the page in your answer book and then write your answer for each number.

(Series 3, 1992, Q3)

Stage 1: Identify the Task

Write the answer for each numbered space.

Now complete the following stages.

Stage 2: Before you Start

Have you ....?

Have you ....?

Mr Browning claimed the (1).............................amount for all three months whereas (2).............................the other representatives, (3).............................Miss Gaskell, claimed (4).............................amounts for each month. The (5).............................total claim was from Mr Rossetti and the (6).............................total claim from Mr Keats who claimed (7).............................for September. (8).............................claim was submitted by Mr Hardy for August. Claims for September have not yet been received from (9).............................representatives. Total combined expenses were higher in (10).............................than in any other month. Mr Rossetti's expenses in July and August exceeded those of all the other representatives combined. The (11).............................monthly total was in September. This figure was only about (12).............................of the total (13).............................which was (14).............................in July. The current quarterly average is (15)............................., which is about one (16).............................more than the average for the (17).............................period a year (18)............................. In fact the current quarterly average is (19) .... higher than the average for the (20).............................of last year.

NAME	JULY	AUGUST	SEPTEMBER
Mr Browning	300	300	300
Mr Hardy	2,500	nil	2,850
Miss Eliot	1,100	950	n/a
Mr Rossetti	5,000	3,800	n/a
Miss Gaskell	700	500	500
Mr Keats	nil	nil	700
TOTALS	**9,600**	**5,500**	**4,350**
Quarterly Average	6,483		
Quarterly Average for same period last year.	4,480	Annual Average for last year.	5,800

(n/a - not available)

Gap-Fills

Stage 3: Write the Answers

Stage 4: Check your Work ☑

Checklist: Gap-Fills

1. Have you completed the task? ☐
2. Have you clearly numbered your answers? ☐
3. Have you found words for all the gaps? ☐
4. Have you checked spelling, grammar and punctuation? ☐

SECTION 5

Practice 5

Situation: One Saturday afternoon in a shopping centre, several shoppers, chosen at random were asked what was the most important feature of a large store.

Task: Study the figures below and complete the text. Only one word or number goes in each space. Write the answers in your answer book.

(Series 3, 1991, Q3)

Now complete the following stages.

Stage 1: Identify the Task

....

Stage 2: Before you Start

Have you .... ?

Have you .... ?

Of the 374 shoppers, more than (1).............................were women and the features they mentioned can be (2).............................down into four broad categories: staff, products, store and price, although this last would include methods of payment, ie (3).............................of credit cards. Any (4).............................manager thinking of a customer-(5).............................programme will be pleased to see that friendly staff came out (6).............................of the list and (7).............................of service (8)............................. second with 52, although for the men (9).............................a well-laid out store was (10).............................important. It is interesting, however, that 6 people preferred to be (11).............................alone to browse, and that (12).............................women than men valued (13).............................service.

As far as the product range was concerned (14).............................seemed to be more important than either low prices or high quality. This category (products) could also include special offers, although it is not clear from the answer whether people wanted money-off offers or 2 for the (15).............................of 1. (Special offers, (16).............................were nevertheless considered (17).............................important than low prices by women.)

With regard to the store itself men were much more impressed by the (18).............................than the decoration, perhaps suggesting that they want to get the shopping done (19)............................., but a spacious store was valued (20).............................by men and women.

	MEN	WOMEN	TOTAL
friendly staff	23	40	63
speedy service at tills/checkout	26	26	52
wide range of products	14	30	44
well laid out store	30	13	43
lower prices	8	26	34
high quality goods	12	19	31
personal service from assistants	5	23	28
frequent special offers	13	10	23
a spacious store	11	11	22
accepts credit/store cards	12	2	14
attractive decoration	2	12	14
assistants who let you browse	5	1	6
TOTAL	161	213	374

Gap-Fills

Stage 3:   Write the Answers

Stage 4:   Check your Work ☑

Checklist: Gap-Fills

1   Have you completed the task? ☐
2   Have you clearly numbered your answers? ☐
3   Have you found words for all the gaps? ☐
4   Have you checked spelling, grammar and punctuation? ☐

SECTION 5

Practice 6

Situation: The bar charts show you the population and population density for the twelve countries that belong to the European Community and for three other countries.

Task: Study the bar charts carefully and complete the statements below. Only one word or number goes in each space. **Write the numbers 1 - 20 in your answer book and write your answers next to each number.**

Note: *Population density means the average number of people who live in each square kilometre.*
(Series 3, 1990, Q3)

Now complete the following stages.

Stage 1: Identify the Task

....

Stage 2: Before you Start

Have you .... ?

Have you .... ?

The bar chart shows that the (1).............................population of the twelve EC countries is (2).............................than that of the USSR or the USA. Of the EC countries, FR Germany has the (3).............................population and Italy, the United Kingdom and France have populations which are approximately (4)............................. In the EC, (5).............................countries have populations of below 10 million, the (6).............................being Luxembourg. The population of Japan is about (7).............................that of the most heavily-populated EC country and the country with the (8).............................population, (9).............................to the bar chart, is the USSR.

There are as (10).............................as 320 people per square kilometre in Japan but the Netherlands has an even (11).............................population density, (12).............................by Belgium and (13)............................. In the EC, Ireland seems to be the (14).............................crowded country and of the larger countries in the EC, Spain has a comparatively (15).............................population density of (16).............................people per square kilometre, but even that seems high compared to the population density of the (17).............................which is (18).............................12 per square kilometre. The (19).............................population density for (20).............................the EC countries is 168 people per square kilometre.

European Community of the 12 (EUR 12)	Population in Millions		Density per km2	
	FR Germany	61.4	245	
	Italy	57.1	189	
	United Kingdom	56.6	231	
	France	55.2	101	
	Spain	38.6	76	
	The Netherlands	14.5	353	
	Portugal	10.2	111	
	Belgium	9.9	323	
	Greece	9.9	76	
	Denmark	5.1	119	
	Ireland	3.5	51	
	Luxembourg	0.4	141	
	EUR 12	322.4	168	
	USSR	278.8	12	
	USA	239.3	26	
	Japan	120.8	320	

Gap-Fills

Stage 3: Write the Answers

Stage 4: Check your Work ☑
Checklist: Gap-Fills
1 Have you completed the task? ☐
2 Have you clearly numbered your answers? ☐
3 Have you found words for all the gaps? ☐
4 Have you checked spelling, grammar and punctuation? ☐

SECTION 5

Practice 7

Situation: You work in the travel and tourism business and have recently studied some government statistics to see if they contain information which is useful to your company.

Task: **Study the table opposite and complete the statements that follow.** You will sometimes have to write a number (eg 9.8) and sometimes a word or phrase (eg Western Europe).

Note: *Copy numbers 1 - 20 as a list in your answer book and write your answers next to the numbers.*
(Series 4, 1990, Q3)

Now complete the following stages.
Stage 1: Identify the Task

....

Stage 2: Before you Start

Have you .... ?

Have you .... ?

The total number of visits to the UK in 1985 was (1) .... million, of which (2) .... were for business purposes. In 1985 there were about (3) .... times more visits in total (4) .... in 1965. The increase was mainly in (5) .... visits, which rose (6) .... 2.8 million in 1965 to 11.5 million in 1985, an increase of about (7) .... per cent. There were, in 1985, 3.8 million visits by North American residents, and about (8) .... as many visits by residents of Western Europe. The number of visits by people who do not come from North America or Western Europe was between (9) .... and (10) .... times greater in 1985 than in 1965.

If we look at the number of visits abroad by UK residents, we see that the biggest increase has been in visits to (11) ...., which have multiplied (12) .... times. However, (13) .... has always been the most popular destination for UK residents. The number of visits by UK residents to places other (14) .... North America and Western Europe (15) .... 100 per cent between 1965 and 1975 and almost (16) .... again between 1975 and 1984.

In 1985 foreign visitors to Britain spent (17) .... money in the UK than UK visitors spent overseas, although this was not true of the (18) .... year. It is clear from the table that there was a small (19) .... in the number of overseas visits by UK residents in 1985 compared with (20) ....

Visits to the UK by Overseas Residents	1965	1975	1984	1985
number of visits	3.6	9.5	13.6	14.5
total business	0.8	1.8	2.9	3.0
total leisure	2.8	7.7	10.7	11.5
total by North American residents	0.9	1.9	3.3	3.8
total by residents of Western Europe	2.2	5.8	7.6	7.9
total other residents	0.5	1.7	2.8	2.8
number of nights	67.6	128.5	154.5	167.7

Visits abroad by UK Residents	1965	1975	1984	1985
number of visits	6.5	12.0	22.1	21.8
total business	0.8	1.8	3.2	3.3
total leisure	5.7	10.2	18.9	18.5
total to North America	0.1	0.5	0.9	0.9
total to Western Europe	5.9	10.5	19.4	19.1
total to other destinations	0.5	1.0	1.8	1.8
number of nights	96.4	164.6	277.5	270.9
money spent in UK by overseas residents (£)	192.0	1218.0	4614.0	5451.0
money spent abroad by UK residents (£)	290.0	917.0	4663.0	4877.0
UK balance on travel account (£)	-98.0	+301.0	-49.0	+574.0

(all figures are in millions)

SECTION 5

Stage 3:   Write the Answers

Stage 4:   Check your Work ☑

Checklist: Gap-Fills

1. Have you completed the task? ☐
2. Have you clearly numbered your answers? ☐
3. Have you found words for all the gaps? ☐
4. Have you checked spelling, grammar and punctuation? ☐

Gap-Fills

Practice 8

Situation: The timetable on the next page shows changes to British Airways flights from Heathrow and Gatwick.

Task: Study the timetable carefully and complete the statements. Do not write the statements in your answer book. **Write the numbers 1-20 in your book and write only the answer next to each number.**

(Series 2, 1992, Q3)

Now complete the following stages.

Stage 1: Identify the Task

....

Stage 2: Before you Start

Have you .... ?

Have you .... ?

1	The airport code for Gatwick is LGW and for Buenos Aires is ....
2	The Heathrow to Harare flights arrive at ....
3	LOS is the code for the airport in ....
4	The Sunday flight from Buenos Aires departs at ....
5	There are flights from Gatwick to Accra on Wednesdays, Sundays and ....
6	The service to Los Angeles leaves from Heathrow's Terminal ....
7	HRE is the code for the airport in ....
8	There are .... flights per week to Tokyo than to Hong Kong.
9	Flights to Tehran leave at .... on Sundays.
10	Kuwait to London flights arrive at 15.55 on ....
11	All flights to Lagos are now ....
12	All services to Tokyo are non-stop during the ....
13	There are .... flights to Buenos Aires every
14	....
15	Flights to Orlando leave at .... on Mondays,
16	from ....
17	There are .... flights a day
18	from .... to Los Angeles.
19	There are .... non-stop services per week from Heathrow
20	to Kuwait from ....

121

SECTION 5

SCHEDULE NEWS	**The London Gatwick - Los Angeles** service will transfer to London Heathrow Terminal 4, providing a new double daily service from Heathrow (LHR).					
NORTH AMERICA	LHR-LAX	Daily	Dep	1230	Arr	1530
		Daily	Dep	1530	Arr	1830
	LAX-LHR	Daily	Dep	1800	Arr	1225
		Daily	Dep	2030	Arr	1500

Gatwick Orlando flights are increased from 2 to 3 weekly.

LGW-ORL	Tue/Thu	Dep	1015	Arr	1445
	Mon	Dep	1115	Arr	1545
ORL-LGW	Tue/Thu	Dep	1715	Arr	0610
	Mon	Dep	1745	Arr	0640

AFRICA — **Lagos** moves this winter to daily non-stop, omitting the one weekly one-stop flight included in last winter's schedule.

LGW-LOS	Daily	Dep	1225	Arr	1950
LOS-LGW	Daily	Dep	2355	Arr	0520

Harare services increased from 2 to 3 weekly.

LHR-HRE	Mon/Wed/Fri	Dep	2115	Arr	0910
HRE-LHR	Tue/Thu/Sat	Dep	2200	Arr	0610

Accra increased from 2 to 3 weekly.

LGW-ACC	Wed/Sun	Dep	1140	Arr	2000
	Thu	Dep	2350	Arr	0620
ACC-LGW	Fri	Dep	0800	Arr	1645
	Wed/Sun	Dep	2140	Arr	0615

FAR EAST — **Tokyo** services are increasing from 12 to 13 per week, and all services this winter are non-stop.

LHR-TYO	Daily	Dep	1200	Arr	0855
	Daily, ex-Wed	Dep	1430	Arr	1125
TYO-LHR	Daily	Dep	1100	Arr	1455
	Daily, ex-Thu	Dep	1355	Arr	1750

Heathrow - Hong Kong upgraded from 9 to 12 weekly.

LHR-HKG	Tue/Fri/Sat	Dep	1405	Arr	1050
	Thu/Sat	Dep	2000	Arr	1905
	Daily	Dep	2115	Arr	1800
HKG-LHR	Fri/Sun	Dep	2120	Arr	0700
	Wed/Sat/Sun	Dep	2215	Arr	0445
	Daily	Dep	2230	Arr	0500

SOUTH AMERICA — **Buenos Aires** increased from 2 to 3 weekly.

LHR-BUE	Tue/Thu	Dep	2155	Arr	1035
	Sat	Dep	2155	Arr	1045
BUE-LHR	Wed	Dep	1335	Arr	0725
	Sun	Dep	1345	Arr	0745
	Fri	Dep	1355	Arr	0745

MIDDLE EAST — **Kuwait** remains at 3 weekly - continued from Summer 91. 2 services are non-stop from October 91.

LHR-KWI	Tue/Sat	Dep	1030	Arr	2020
	Mon	Dep	2000	Arr	0750
KWI-LHR	Wed/Sun	Dep	0145	Arr	0625
	Tue	Dep	0915	Arr	1555

Tehran is back for its first winter season since 1985 - reintroduced July 91.

LHR-THR	Sun	Dep	1240	Arr	0025
	Wed	Dep	1335	Arr	0120
THR-LHR	Mon	Dep	0150	Arr	0725
	Thu	Dep	0245	Arr	0820

Winter schedule commences 28 October 1992.

Gap-Fills

Stage 3: Write the Answers

Stage 4: Check your Work ☑

Checklist: Gap-Fills

1. Have you completed the task? ☐
2. Have you clearly numbered your answers? ☐
3. Have you found words for all the gaps? ☐
4. Have you checked spelling, grammar and punctuation? ☐

SECTION 5

Practice 9

Opposite you will find a table containing information on insurance premiums for electrical goods for 2 and 4 years. Use this to complete the statements below.

(Series 4, 1991, Q3)

Now complete the following stages.

Stage 1: Identify the Task

....

Stage 2: Before you Start

Have you .... ?

Have you .... ?

A Complete the gaps with **more** or **less**.

1 Insuring a colour TV for 4 years costs .... than £40.

2 A compact disc player can be insured for .... than £50.

3 An audio system, costing .... than £500 can be insured for £24.95.

4 A camera costing £600 can be insured for no .... than £27.95.

5 Video camera insurance for 4 years costs .... than £40.

B Complete the gaps with information from the table.

6 The most expensive premium quoted is for a ....

7 The .... premium for 2 years' insurance is £97.95.

8 .... items can be insured for £34.95.

9 Insurance for 2 years for a £400 camera costs ....

10 A portable audio would cost .... for 2 years' insurance.

C Compare the premiums for the following items. State whether the first is **higher** or **lower** than the second.

Two Years

11 Camcorder compared with CD player.
12 £400 audio system compared with £400 camera.
13 Colour TV compared with audio system plus CD.
14 Stereo radio compared with CD player.
15 £100 camera compared with mono TV.

Four Years

16 Clock radio/cassette/MTV compared with portable audio.
17 CD player compared with video camera.
18 Colour TV compared with CD player.
19 Microwave compared with £400 audio system plus CD.
20 VCR compared with camcorder.

PRODUCTS AND PRICES	INSURANCE PREMIUM FOR FOUR YEARS	INSURANCE PREMIUM FOR TWO YEARS
Colour Television	£41.95	£30.95
Mono Television	£21.95	£14.95
Combined CTV and Video Recorder	£119.95	£79.95
Video Cassette Recorder	£84.95	£61.95
Portable Audio	£23.95	£17.95
Stereo Radio Cassette	£32.95	£24.95
Clock Radio /Cassette/MTV	£34.95	£25.95
Audio System to £500	£32.95	£24.95
Audio System to £1,250	£46.95	£34.95
Audio System including CD to £500	£66.95	£48.95
Audio System including CD to £1,250	£76.95	£58.95
Audio Separates	£23.95	£17.95
Compact Disc Player	£42.95	£31.95
Camera to £250	£21.95	£15.95
Camera to £600	£27.95	£19.95
Video Camera	£58.95	£43.95
Microwave	£34.95	£25.95
Camcorder	£133.95	£97.95

SECTION 5

Stage 3: Write the Answers

Stage 4: Check your Work ☑

Checklist: Gap-Fills

1. Have you completed the task? ☐
2. Have you clearly numbered your answers? ☐
3. Have you found words for all the gaps? ☐
4. Have you checked spelling, grammar and punctuation? ☐

Gap-Fills

Practice 10

Situation: You work for a large British oil company. Recently your company has raised the price of petrol to over £2 per gallon because of a government tax increase. Motorists are not happy about this increase and your company wants to show them that oil companies are not making large profits from the high price of petrol.

Task: You have been given a diagram showing how the price of petrol is calculated. Use information from the diagram to fill in the gaps in the sentences below. **Write your answers in your answer booklet.**

(Series 4, 1988, Q3)

Now complete the following stages.

Stage 1: Identify the Task

....

Stage 2: Before you Start

Have you .... ?

Have you .... ?

1. After the recent 4p tax increase, the price of a gallon of petrol rose from (a)..............................to (b)..........................

2. The petrol itself costs (c)..............................than half of the total price.

3. The oil company buys crude oil for (d)..............................pence per gallon. It costs (e)..............................pence to manufacture the petrol and the company makes only (f) .... pence profit.

4. Petrol stations pay (g)..............................for a gallon of petrol.

5. Petrol stations add (h)..............................pence to the price they pay for the petrol.

6. (i)..............................half of the cost of petrol goes in tax. There are two kinds of tax on petrol (j)..............................and (k)..............................tax.

7. About one-third of the tax is (l)..............................while the remaining two-thirds is (m).............................. The total tax on a gallon of petrol is (n)..............................

8. The motorist now pays (o)..............................pence for a gallon of petrol.

9. 53% of the price of a gallon of petrol goes to (p).............................., 3.5% to (q)..............................and 43.5% goes to (r)..............................

10. So (s)..............................is responsible for the rise in petrol prices, not (t)..............................

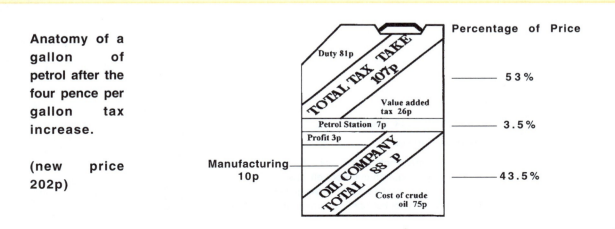

Anatomy of a gallon of petrol after the four pence per gallon tax increase.

(new price 202p)

Duty 81p
TOTAL TAX TAKE 107p
Value added tax 26p
Petrol Station 7p
Profit 3p
Manufacturing 10p
OIL COMPANY TOTAL 88 P
Cost of crude oil 75p

Percentage of Price
53%
3.5%
43.5%

SECTION 5

Stage 3: Write the Answers

Stage 4: Check your Work ☑

Checklist: Gap-Fills

1. Have you completed the task? ☐
2. Have you clearly numbered your answers? ☐
3. Have you found words for all the gaps? ☐
4. Have you checked spelling, grammar and punctuation? ☐

SECTION 6: Forms and Diagrams

Introduction
The type of question using forms and diagrams often occurs in Question 4.

Stage 1: Identify the Task
This type of question normally has some written information (a note, letter, tapescript, etc), and a form or diagram. You are asked to pick out the details required on the form. Do not write on the form. Your answers must be written in your answer book.

Stage 2: How to Complete the Task
You have to decide which details are required on the form and find these in the given information.

The best approach is:
1. Read through the given information and work out what it is about.
2. Look at the form or diagram and see what information is required.
3. Go back to the first question and start answering them one by one.

Remember:
- write your answers in the answer book
- make sure you give the correct details
- if you can't find an answer go on to the next

Stage 3: How to Answer
You should not write on the examination paper and you should not copy the form into your book (unless it says so). You should list the numbers and write your answers next to them. Make sure your answers are clearly numbered, easy to read and that the correct details are with the correct question numbers. If the form says "Please use block capitals" your answer must be in BLOCK CAPITALS too.

Stage 4: Check your Work
Checklist: Forms and Diagrams

The following is a list of points to check when you answer this type of question.
1. Have you completed the task?
2. Have you clearly numbered your answers?
3. Have you answered all the points?
4. Have you checked spelling, grammar and punctuation?

SECTION 6

Practice 1

Situation: You have decided to sell three items that you no longer need. These items are: a large oak bookcase in good condition; a portable electric typewriter (almost new) with its accessories; and a large wooden desk with drawers. You have decided to sell these by advertising in a local newspaper. These items are classified as office equipment and the classification number is S12. You want to get more than £100 for them altogether.

Task: **Complete the form** which you will post to the newspaper. This form enables the newspaper to prepare your advertisements.

Note: You need not copy the whole form into your answer book. **You should write down, in your answer book, the numbers 1 - 18 and place your answer next to each number.** Make up any necessary information.

(Series 4, 1990, Q4)

Stage 1: Identify the Task
Complete the form.

Stage 2: Before you Start
Have you read through **all** the information?
Have you read through the form?

How to Place Your Advertisement (Private For Sale Advertisers only)

To place your ad follow the 4 easy steps below.

Writing Your Ad: Write your ad in BLOCK CAPITALS in the grid below, **one** word or price in each box - A **maximum** of 12 words in the boxes. Start the ad with a descriptive name of the item (eg BIKE) and don't forget your **telephone number and price of the item(s)**.

Please insert the classification number of the item(s) here (1).............................

(2)	(3)	(4)	(5)
(6)	(7)	(8)	(9)
(10)	(11)	(12)	(13)
(14) Tel:			

Price Your Ad: Please price your ad using the price grid below. Please tick the appropriate box.

(15) for items totalling £25   £2   for items totalling under £50   £5

       for items totalling under £100   £8   for items totalling over £100   £10

Paying for Your Ad: Ads can be paid for by Access, Visa or Cheque (all cheques must be supported by a cheque card number). Please also print your name and address below.

(16) Access/Visa Card Number ....   (17) Name...

     Cheque enclosed/Cheque Card Number   (18) Address..

     ....

Note: 'Ad' = advertisement

Forms and Diagrams

Stage 3: Write the Answers

1	S12		11	ELECTRIC
2	OFFICE		12	TYPEWRITER
3	EQUIPMENT		13	£20
4	LARGE		14	Tel 0386 54249
5	OAK		15	£10
6	BOOKCASE		16	Access Card Number 01364892
7	£50		17	JOE BLOGGS
8	WOODEN		18	14 HIGH STREET PERTH SCOTLAND
9	DESK			
10	£35			

Stage 4: Check your Work ✓

Checklist: Forms and Diagrams

1. Have you completed the task? ✓
2. Have you clearly numbered your answers? ✓
3. Have you answered all the points? ✓
4. Have you checked spelling, grammar and punctuation? ✓

SECTION 6

Practice 2

Situation: You and your Sales Director, Jack Hughes, have been invited to speak at the forthcoming International Sales Congress in Novo Castillo, Spain.

Task: Use the information from the note below to complete the form below **for your colleague**. Do **not** copy the form in the answer book. Write the numbers in your answer book and put your answers next to the appropriate number.

(Series 4, 1992, Q4)

Stage 1: Identify the Task
Complete the form.

Stage 2: Before you Start
Have you read through **all** the information?
Have you read through the form?

Tel: 0303 26459
Fax: 0303 26450

Crowe, Dugdale, Deakin
Typewriter Manufacturers
Kargush Tower
21 Meadowcourt Avenue
FOLKESTONE   CT93 9FE

14th

For the Congress

It's practical again. Like the one I did at Neuburg; remember, "Dealing with European Competition?" But this time I want to widen the scope, so not "European" but "International".

I'll need 2 computers, a flip chart, and a portable cassette player.

No more than a dozen people: they'll have to sign up. And as it's a workshop I won't need a chair.

Jack

Directors: P Cartwright, M Landon, R Blane, C Foster, J Hughes.

Conference Speaker

Name: (1).................................
Title: (2).................................
Company: (3).................................
Address: (4).................................
Telephone: (5).................................
Type of Business: (6).................................

Please use block capitals.

Title of Presentation: (7).................................
Format: (8).................................
Maximum no of Participants: (9).................................
(only for workshop)
Equipment required: (10).................................
Do you require a Chairman? (11).................................

132

Forms and Diagrams

Stage 3: Write the Answers

1	JACK HUGHES	7	INTERNATIONAL COMPETITION
2	SALES DIRECTOR	8	WORKSHOP
3	CROWE, DUGDALE & DEAKIN	9	12
4	KARGUSH TOWER 21 MEADOWCOURT AVENUE FOLKESTONE CT93 9FE	10	2 COMPUTERS FLIP CHART PORTABLE CASSETTE PLAYER
5	0303 26459	11	NO
6	TYPEWRITER MANUFACTURERS		

Now complete the following stage.

Stage 4: Check your Work ☑

Checklist: Forms and Diagrams

1. Have you completed the task? ☐
2. Have you clearly numbered your answers? ☐
3. Have you answered all the points? ☐
4. Have you checked spelling, grammar and punctuation? ☐

SECTION 6

Practice 3

Situation: While waiting for a connecting flight at Heathrow last week your boss, Gerry Hitchens, met a potential customer and recorded the details on his mini-cassette recorder.

Task: Use the information in the transcript below to complete the contact form below **in his name**.

Note: *Do not copy the form.* **Write the numbers 1-14 in your answer book and put the answers next to each number.**

(Series 3, 1992, Q4)

Stage 1: Identify the Task
Complete the form.

Stage 2: Before you Start
Have you read through **all** the information?
Have you read through the form?

"............... then there was Peter Drews and his wife Anne. The latter is the one to write to (personally, not a standard letter) as she's the Chief Buyer in the Purchasing Department.

The company is Lancaster Computers but they also have interests in the USA. At the moment she's based in Manchester, Aston Tower, 145 McParland Avenue.

I've asked her to drop in when she's next in London - maybe to see Vic because I can't visit her as I'm out of the country for the next couple of weeks. Meantime, send her a brochure as well on the 3 machines she wanted to know about: the AD 40, the Empress and the Ultra-Clean Emsworth. Oh yes, I've just checked her card and the post code is MVR 14U. Offer her a special price if she takes all 3 machines at the same time."

Contact made by: (1) ....
At: (2) .... Date: (3) ....

Contact
Name: (4) ....
Company: (5) ....
Address: (6) ....
....
Department: (7) ....
Position: (8) ....
Interested in: (9) ....

Action
Write: YES/NO (10)   Visit: YES/NO (13)   Send Brochure: YES/NO (11)
Send Quote: YES/NO (12)   Invite: YES/NO (14)

Forms and Diagrams

Now complete the following stages.

Stage 3: Write the Answers

Stage 4: Check your Work ☑

Checklist: Forms and Diagrams

1 Have you completed the task? ☐
2 Have you clearly numbered your answers? ☐
3 Have you answered all the points? ☐
4 Have you checked spelling, grammar and punctuation? ☐

135

SECTION 6

Practice 4

Situation: On the second day of the trade fair mentioned below, your boss, Peter Kirk, made several contacts. For one he had no contact form but made the following notes.

Task: Use the notes to **complete the form** in his name.

Note: *You do not need to copy the whole form into your answer book.* **You should write down, in your answer book, the numbers 1-14 and place your answer next to each number. Write in block capitals.**

(Series 2, 1991, Q4)

Stage 1: Identify the Task

Complete the form.

Now complete the following stages.

Stage 2: Before you Start

Have you .... ?

Have you .... ?

BARBICAN Interop Trade Fair: 14-16 Jan

Last of the day. Just before leaving Dr James or John Pickering. Works for Arkon US. The Marketing dept.

Some sort of Account Executive. Not worth visiting or taking out for lunch - he's going back to the US next week.

Wanted to know what we could do in the way of intercom systems, alarms and master clocks.

Said I'd send him details. No harm in putting in a quote.

Note: He's staying with the Commercial Attache at the London US Embassy in Grosvenor Square, W1 until he leaves. Must also write to thank him for the other contacts he recommended.

Contact made by: (1) ....
At: (2) .... Date: (3) ....
Contact
Name: (4) ....
Company: (5) ....
Address: (6) ....
....
Department: (7) ....
Position: (8) ....
Interested in: (9) ....

Action
Write: YES/NO (10)   Visit: YES/NO (13)   Send Brochure: YES/NO (11)
Send Quote: YES/NO (12)   USE BLOCK CAPITALS   Invite: YES/NO (14)

Forms and Diagrams

Stage 3: Write the Answers

Stage 4: Check your Work ☑

Checklist: Forms and Diagrams

1. Have you completed the task? ☐
2. Have you clearly numbered your answers? ☐
3. Have you answered all the points? ☐
4. Have you checked spelling, grammar and punctuation? ☐

SECTION 6

Practice 5

Situation: You are responsible for the ordering of office supplies. You have received the following memo from your Office Manager.

MEMO

To: Supplies Officer
From: Office Manager
Subject: Order Form (attached)
Date: Thursday 3rd May

Following the recent meeting of the Planning Committee, could you please make some alterations to the order that we discussed recently. Please order three-drawer filing cabinets - this will increase the price to £339. We also need twenty FAX rolls and sixty calculators and you should change the order to two shredders and two binders which will come to £240 and £398 respectively. We do not need a postal scale, so please delete it entirely and substitute one Overhead Projector (£249) - please check the item code in your catalogue. Please specify that the typists' chairs should be red (and we need 20), the filing cabinets should be grey-green and the wall clocks must be pine - I think the code for these is J1234, by the way. This will bring the order to £3851 and entitle us to a 10% discount and free delivery, giving a total of £3466.

Task: Copy the following form into your answer book, making all the corrections as advised by the Office Manager in his memo. Complete every part of the order form. You will receive marks for each complete and correct line

(Series 2, 1990, Q4)

Now complete the following stages.

Stage 1: Identify the Task

....

Stage 2: Before you Start

Have you ....?

Have you ....?

ORDER FORM

	ITEM CODE	DESCRIPTION	QUANTITY	PRICE (£)
1	F1234	2-Drawer Filing Cabinet	4	239
2	F1111	Typists' Chairs (grey)	10	550
3	F1627	M1 Fax	1	575
4	S6198	Fax Rolls	10	60
5	F1588	Calculators	20	200
6	S5467	Binder	1	199
7	J2135	Postal Scale	1	225
8	F1360	Shredder	1	120
9	J2134	Wall Clock	2	50
10	S5674	Flipchart	3	180

Sub Total	2398
Less Discount	NIL
Delivery Charge	35
TOTAL	2433

Stage 3: Write the Answers

Stage 4: Check your Work ☑

Checklist: Forms and Diagrams

1. Have you completed the task? ☐
2. Have you clearly numbered your answers? ☐
3. Have you answered all the points? ☐
4. Have you checked spelling, grammar and punctuation? ☐

SECTION 6

Practice 6

Situation: You are James Kirk, Personnel Manager of a large firm of coffee and tea importers, and you receive the note below from a colleague in the Sales Department.

Task: Use the information in the note to complete the registration form below. Do **not** copy the form into your answer book: write the number and your answer next to the number.

(Series 2, 1992, Q4)

Now complete the following stages.

Stage 1: Identify the Task

....

Stage 2: Before you Start

Have you .... ?

Have you .... ?

Carsten Bros
Lake View Tower
Meadowcourt Avenue
LONDON   SE3 9EU

Tel: 081-318-5633
Fax: 081-318-1812

Jim

I've decided to let Jane, my PA, go on the Executive Secretary Programme as a residential member at the Metropole, Brighton.

As she's on holiday at the moment can you book a place for her. She's not back for 2 weeks so give your name as a contact. Arrange payment on account as usual.

Thanks.
John

PS   Although she's married she wants Ms Heyworth on her badge.

| Registration Form | Complete in Block Capitals | Tick where appropriate |

(1) Course .... (2) Location .... (3) Mrs ☐ Miss ☐ Ms ☐

(4) Surname .... (5) Christian Name .... (6) Job Title ....

(7) Department .... (8) Company .... (9) Address ....

(10) Phone ....

(11) Type of Business .... (12) Person to be contacted in case of query.
....

(13) Is accommodation required?   Y ☐   N ☐

(14) Payment   Cheque Enclosed ☐   Account ☐

                   Send Invoice ☐   Credit Card ☐

Forms and Diagrams

Stage 3:   Write the Answers

Stage 4:   Check your Work ☑

Checklist: Forms and Diagrams

1 Have you completed the task? ☐
2 Have you clearly numbered your answers? ☐
3 Have you answered all the points? ☐
4 Have you checked spelling, grammar and punctuation? ☐

141

SECTION 6

Practice 7

Situation: You have just interviewed Richard Blane, Course Director of the Management Consultancy Institute.

Task: Use the transcript of the recording you made below to complete the organisational chart below. Do **not** write on the chart. Write the numbers 1 to 20 in your answer book and put the answer next to the appropriate number.

(Series 2, 1993, Q4)

Now complete the following stages.

Stage 1: Identify the Task

....

Stage 2: Before you Start

Have you .... ?

Have you .... ?

"........... well I have overall responsibility for the courses but I do have three assistants; Mike Foster runs the part-time courses, John Kane the intensive courses and Brendan Charles is the in-company supremo.

All the secretarial stuff is handled by Paula Essex who reports to the Administration Manager. He also supervises Ralph Charrer, who's the Security Chief.

The Institute Director is Dr Martin, who's tough, especially when he deals with the Foundation Council on our behalf. It's difficult because they're in Amsterdam. His PA is Melissa Andrews.

If you want to see someone about marketing strategy then you need Jack Hughes. The individual areas are looked after by Alan Deakin (UK), Vic Crowe and Jim Dugdale. The latter does Europe."

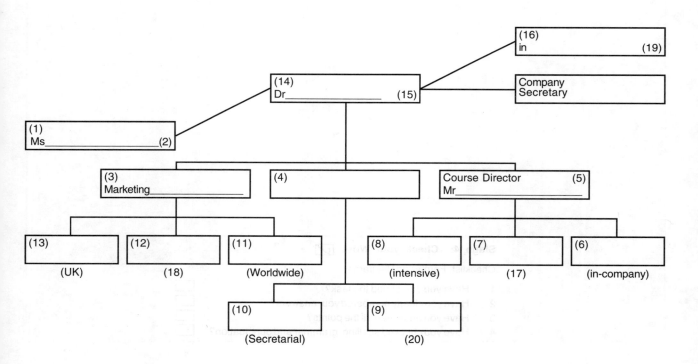

Forms and Diagrams

Stage 3: Write the Answers

Stage 4: Check your Work ☑
Checklist: Forms and Diagrams
1. Have you completed the task? ☐
2. Have you clearly numbered your answers? ☐
3. Have you answered all the points? ☐
4. Have you checked spelling, grammar and punctuation? ☐

SECTION 6

Practice 8

Situation: Your manager has asked you to complete the plan of the supermarket layout opposite.

Task: Read the directions below and decide which letter on the plan each direction refers to. Do **not** write on the diagram. Write the numbers 1 to 20 in your answer book and put the appropriate **letter** next to each number.

(Series 1, 1993, Q4)

Now complete the following stages.

Stage 1: Identify the Task

....

Stage 2: Before you Start

Have you .... ?

Have you .... ?

1	The bacon is next to the sausages.
2	The cereals are between the biscuits and the sugar.
3	The coffee is next to the fruit.
4	The crisps are between the nuts and the snacks.
5	The delicatessen is immediately to the right of the checkouts.
6	The entrance to the cold store is between the meat and the ethnic foods.
7	The entrance to the warehouse is next to the beers.
8	The flour is next to the cake mixes.
9	The exotic vegetables are next to the plants.
10	...and the ordinary vegetables are opposite.
11	The milk is between the sausages and the dairy produce.
12	The oils are opposite the salad dressing.
13	The pet foods are opposite the sugar.
14	The sandwiches are immediately to the left of the entrance.
15	The soft drinks are opposite the tomatoes.
16	The soup is between the pasta and the beans.
17	The tea is next to the coffee.
18	The toilet rolls are next to the plastics.
19	The tomatoes are next to the beans.
20	The trolleys are immediately to the right of the entrance, as you walk into the store.

Forms and Diagrams

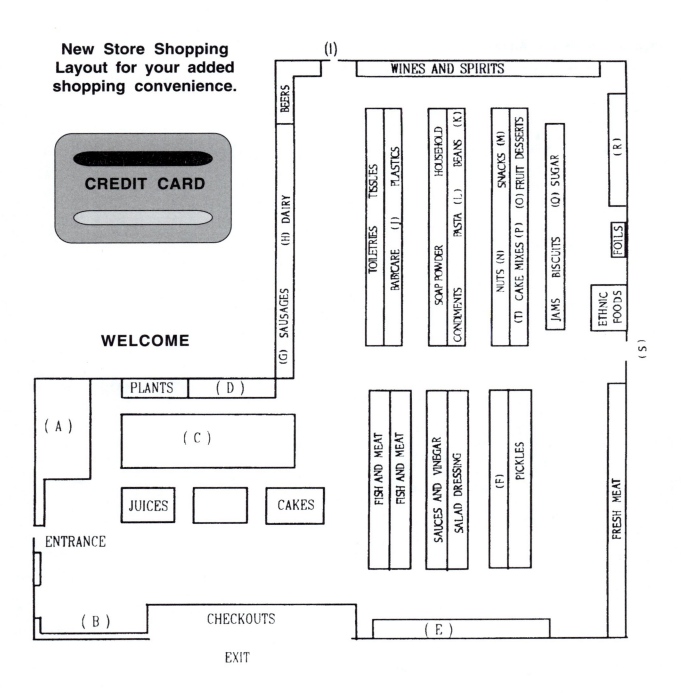

CONVENIENT SHOPPING HOURS

All Day Monday	8am - 6pm
Tuesday to Friday	8am - 8pm
All Day Saturday	8am - 6pm

145

SECTION 6

Stage 3: Write the Answers

Stage 4: Check your Work ☑

Checklist: Forms and Diagrams

1. Have you completed the task? ☐
2. Have you clearly numbered your answers? ☐
3. Have you answered all the points? ☐
4. Have you checked spelling, grammar and punctuation? ☐

Forms and Diagrams

Practice 9

Situation: Over the weekend you make rough plans for your time during the following month.

Task: Use the notes to complete your pocket diary. Do **not** copy the diary into your answer book: write the day number in brackets( ), not the full date - followed by your answer. Remember that it is a pocket diary, so your answers should be brief.
If there is no information for a particular day, you must write the word "free" after the number.

Note: *Make only one entry for each day.*
(Series 1, 1992, Q4)

Now complete the following stages.

Stage 1: Identify the Task

....

Stage 2: Before you Start

Have you .... ?

Have you .... ?

Finance Committee meeting at 2.30pm every Wednesday.

Staff appraisals at 10.00am every other Monday, starting on the 10th.

The Head Office is sending auditors, 3 of them, on the last two days of the month. (Glad I have a day's holiday on the 25th!)

Lunch with Peter on the 4th. Table's already booked 12.30pm.

Essential   Must finish the review of Kirk's article - it's due in Glasgow on 21st. I'll fax it the day before!

Andy is leaving on the 14th so I must remember to write a few notes for the speech when I give him the present. I'll get Carol to check his service here. She can do that on the Thursday before.

Staff Inductions   Three people on the 6th & 7th
                      10 - 4 both days

Tomorrow   Cancel the staff meeting which was provisionally fixed for the 10th.

147

SECTION 6

199__

SAT	1	
SUN	2	
MON	3	(1)
TUE	4	(2)
WED	5	(3)
THU	6	(4)
FRI	7	(5)
SAT	8	
SUN	9	
MON	10	(6)
TUE	11	(7)
WED	12	(8)
THU	13	(9)
FRI	14	(10)
SAT	15	
SUN	16	
MON	17	(11)
TUE	18	(12)
WED	19	(13)
THU	20	(14)
FRI	21	(15)
SAT	22	
SUN	23	
MON	24	(16)
TUE	25	(17)
WED	26	(18)
THU	27	(19)
FRI	28	(20)
SAT	29	
SUN	30	

Forms and Diagrams

Stage 3: Write the Answers 149

Stage 4: Check your Work ☑

Checklist: Forms and Diagrams

1. Have you completed the task? ☐
2. Have you clearly numbered your answers? ☐
3. Have you answered all the points? ☐
4. Have you checked spelling, grammar and punctuation? ☐

SECTION 6

Practice 10

Situation: Below there is a note from your boss, James T Kirk, to you about investing in more computers. Use the information to complete the "request for information" form opposite in his name.

Task: Do not write on the form. Write your answers in the answer book. You need not copy the whole form into your answer book. You should write down, in your answer book, the numbers 1-15 and place your answers next to each number. Make up any necessary information.

(Series 1, 1991, Q4)

Now complete the following stages.

Stage 1: Identify the Task

....

Stage 2: Before you Start

Have you .... ?

Have you .... ?

Kirk and Stevens
Brewers of Distinction
51 Marischal Road
LONDON SE19 7KS

Tel: 081-318-5634

14th

John

I think it's time we got some more computers to add to the one my secretary's got and the one in accounts. I'd like one for a start. And then one/two for warehousing for stock control. I really need one for presentations and design.

We're happy with the IBM and the Squirrel but we can get some info about others. At the moment we can go up to about £6,000 for 3 machines.

Can you look after this?

Thanks.

Jim

Forms and Diagrams

1 Do you already have any computers?

☐ None   ☐ 1   ☐ 2-5
☐ 5-10   ☐ more

2 If yes, are you satisfied that they are appropriate for your business?

YES/NO

3 Which computers are they?

☐ Commodore   ☐ IBM   ☐ Amstrad

☐ Olivetti   Other (Please specify) ....

4 Who would use the extra computers?

☐ Self   ☐ Accountant   ☐ Secretary   ☐ Sales

☐ MD   Other (please specify) ....

5 For what purpose?

☐ Stock Control   ☐ Spread Sheet   ☐ Accounting

☐ Design   ☐ Better Presentation

6 How many business computers are you considering investing in at present?

☐ 1   ☐ 1-5   ☐ 5-10   ☐ 10+

7 Number of employees.

☐ 1-5   ☐ 6-10   ☐ 11-20
☐ 21-50   ☐ 51+

8 What is your computer budget?

☐ £300   ☐ £301-£500   ☐ £501-£1000
☐ £1001-£2000   ☐ £2001+

Complete the section below in block capitals.

9 Name ....

10 Position ....

11 Company ....

12 Address ....

   ....

   ....

13 Post Code ....

14 Telephone ....

15 Type of Business ....

SECTION 6

Stage 3: Write the Answers

Stage 4: Check your Work ☑

Checklist: Forms and Diagrams
1. Have you completed the task? ☐
2. Have you clearly numbered your answers? ☐
3. Have you answered all the points? ☐
4. Have you checked spelling, grammar and punctuation? ☐

ANSWER KEY

Section 1: Letters

Practice 3

Stage 5: Write the Letter

Tourist Office
19 Eldon Gardens
Perth
PH13 4NL

28th April 1993

Mr M Rees
21 Meadowcourt Road
London
SE3 9EU

Dear Mr Rees

The Tourist Office in Perth is looking for someone to write a short guide to the town and local area. I was given your address by a work colleague, Archie Leach. I am familiar with "The London Book" which you have written and am hoping to find a writer to produce a similar work about Perth.

Ideally the guide would include information about places to visit, places of interest, places of outstanding beauty and also good places to eat.

The payment package would provide a sum in advance, cover all expenses during the research period and the author would receive 10% of every book sold.

If you are interested, I would suggest we arrange a date to discuss details.

I look forward to hearing from you.

Yours sincerely

(your signature)
(printed name)

ANSWER KEY

Practice 4

Stage 4: Group/Order Relevant Information

1. New "Special Intensive Course for Managers."
2. Course was developed because of Single Market.
3. Course will contain:
   - trade policies of other countries
   - cultural differences
   - importance of language training.
4. Course will take place from October 10th - 15th 1992.
5. At the Grande Hotel, Black Street, London W1.
6. £100 per person, per day.
7. Brochure enclosed for more details.
8. If interested, contact address in brochure.

Stage 5: Write the Letter

European Management Consultancy
21 High Street
London   W1

26th June 1992

The Personnel Manager
Funtime Computers
19 Market Street
London   W1

Dear Sir/Madam

I am writing to inform you of our new "Special Intensive Course for Managers." This course was developed to improve company chances in the Single Market. The course will contain seminars and workshops on many subjects including:

- trade policies of other countries
- cultural differences
- importance of language training.

The course will take place from October 10th to 15th at the Grande Hotel, Black Street, London W1 and will cost £100 per person per day. For exact details of content please read the enclosed brochure at your leisure.

If you are interested or require further information please contact me.

I look forward to hearing form you.

Yours faithfully

(your signature)
(printed name)
Marketing Assistant

Practice 5

Stage 3: Identify Relevant Information

- visit HQ for 2 days

- confirm dates and arrival times (Mon 12th July, 7.45pm)

- Tim Taylor, Sales Manager - will meet at airport (he will have a sign)

- stay at Maritime Hotel, 21 Front View, Newcastle

- visit includes:
    - meeting with Marketing Manager, Tom Brown - Marketing Strategies
    - sales report on UK by Tim Taylor
    - trip to Bamburgh Castle

- take him back to Airport

Stage 4: Group/Order Relevant Information

1   Confirm dates for visit.

2   Confirm arrival times (Mon 12th July, 7.45pm).

3   Tim Taylor, Sales Manager will collect him. He will have a sign.

4   Outline of visit:

    Day 1   Meeting at HQ with Marketing Manager, Tom Brown
                     Marketing Strategies
                       Lunch and Sales
                       Report on UK in Afternoon

    Day 2   Trip to Bamburgh Castle and a game of Golf.

5   Return to Airport for check-in time.

6   Hotel name and address.

ANSWER KEY

Stage 5: Write the Letter

Aegis Insurance Co
24 High Street
Newcastle   NE46 4AA
England

30th June 1993

Dr Glen Turner
Aegis Insurance Co
Lake View Tower
264 High Street
Allambie   NSW 2100
Australia

Dear Dr Turner

I am writing to you to confirm the dates for your visit to our headquarters in Newcastle, England. You will arrive on Monday 12th July at 7.45pm in Newcastle International Airport. Our Sales Manager, Tim Taylor will collect you. He will have a card with your name on so you will find him.

The outline of your visit is as follows:

Day 1	7.45am	Tim Taylor will collect you from the hotel and take you to headquarters.
	8.00am	Meeting with Marketing Manager, Tom Brown, about Marketing Strategies.
	12.00-1.00pm	Lunch.
	1.00-5.00pm	Meeting with Tim Taylor about Sales Projections UK/Australia.
		I will take you out in the evening to a restaurant.
Day 2	7.45am	I will collect you from your hotel.
	9.30am	Trip around Bamburgh Castle.
	12.00-2.00pm	Lunch in Alnwick.
	2.00pm	Golf at Slaley Hall.

Tom Brown will collect you on the morning of Day 3, Thursday 15th July, at 6.00am and drive you to the Airport for your check-in time of 6.45am.

The name of the hotel is Maritime Hotel and the telephone number is 091 735 9491.

I look forward to seeing you again.

Yours sincerely

Geoff Pullar

Geoff Pullar
Director of Personnel

Section 1: Letters

Practice 6

Stage 2: Layout

- your company address - Happy Pack Ltd, Trent Industrial Estate, Nottingham, NG7 2BA
- the date - 11th March 1991
- the name and address of the person to whom you are writing - Brown's Coaches, 29 High Street, Beeston, Nottingham, NG2 9RP
- correct salutation - Dear Sirs
- complimentary close - Yours faithfully
- signature/name/position - (your signature and name) Office Manager

Stage 3: Identify Relevant Information

- planning summer's outing
- all office and factory workers
- need quotation from them
- hire of 1 or 2 coaches
- a day trip to Brownley village
- evening meal in Alfreton
- 53 people in total
- leaving our company 8.00am
- returning 10.00pm approximately
- outing on 2nd July

Stage 4: Group/Order Relevant Information

1. Planning summer outing.
2. All office and factory workers.
3. Hire of 1 or 2 coaches.
4. 2nd July.
5. 53 in total.
6. Depart from Happy Pack 8.00am.
7. Trip to Brownley village.
8. Have evening meal in Alfreton.
9. Return to Happy Pack approximately 10.00pm.
10. Need quotation.

Stage 5: Write the Letter

Happy Pack Ltd
Trent Industrial Estate
Nottingham NG7 2BA

11th March 1991

Brown's Coaches
29 High Street
Nottingham   NG2 9RP

Dear Sirs

I work for a large fruit-packing company and am presently planning a summer outing for all our staff and factory workers. I am interested in hiring a coach/es for this outing which is to take place on the 2nd July.

The number of people involved will be 53. Ideally the coach/es would leave our factory at 8.00am and then take them to Brownley village in Sherwood Forest. Staff would go on a guided tour returning to the bus at 5.00pm. They would then go to Alfreton for a meal, returning to our factory at approximately 10.00pm.

I would be grateful if you would send me a quotation and let me know how many coaches will be required.

Yours faithfully

(your signature)
(printed name)
Office Manager

ANSWER KEY

Practice 7

Stage 1: Identify the Task

Write a letter.

Stage 2: Layout

- your company address - Watt's Industrial Supplies, Brighton House, 21-23 Blackwell Street, London, EC3 5PN
- the date - 29th November 1993
- the name and address of the person to whom you are writing
- correct salutation - Dear Regional Manager
- complimentary close - Yours faithfully
- signature/name/position - (your signature and name) Sales Manager Europe

Stage 3: Identify Relevant Information

- annual European three-day Sales Conference due to take place week after next
- postponed until 18th-20th January 1994
- sorry, unforeseen circumstances
- changes to programme are as follows:
  Day 1 Mon 18   2pm-4pm - Jim McBride with European Sales Report.
  Day 2 Tues 19 8am-11.30am - Workshop.
  Day 2 Tues 19 Evening: Dinner with guest speaker Simon Rullerford of MJ Marketing Consultants.
- we will use same hotel
- arrival and departure times as in original programme
- enclose copy of new programme

Stage 4: Group/Order Relevant Information

1. Unforeseen circumstances.
2. Annual European three-day conference due to take place the week after next.
3. Postponed until 18th - 20th January 1994.
4. Arrival and departure times as in original programme.
5. We will use the same hotel (Interopa).
6. Changes to programme are:
   Day 1 Mon 18   2pm-4pm - Jim McBride with European Sales Report.
   Day 2 Tues 19   8am-11.30am - Workshop, Psychology of Selling.
   Day 2 Tues 19   8pm onwards: Dinner with guest speaker Simon Rullerford of MJ Marketing Consultants.
7. Enclose a copy of new programme.
8. Sorry.

Stage 5: Write the Letter

> Watt's Industrial Supplies
> Brighton House
> 21-23 Blackwell Street
> London
> EC3 5PN
>
> 29th November 1993
>
> Dear Regional Manager
>
> Due to unforeseen circumstances, the annual European three-day Sales Conference which was planned to take place the week after next has been postponed until Monday 18th - Wednesday 20th January 1994.
>
> The arrival and departure times will remain as in the original programme and we will use the same hotel (Hotel Interopa).
>
> Please note the following changes to the programme:
>
> Day 1   Monday 18th January 1994 2pm to 4pm
>   Jim McBride will present a report on Sales in Europe.
>
> Day 2   Tuesday 19th January 1994 8am to 11.30am
>   Workshop - Psychology of Selling.
>
> Day 2   Tuesday 19th January 1994 8pm onwards
>   Dinner with guest speaker Simon Rullerford of MJ Marketing Consultants.
>
> I have enclosed a copy of the new programme which contains all of the details of this event. I apologise for the changes and hope this will not cause any inconvenience.
>
> Yours faithfully
>
>
> (your signature)
> (printed name)
> Sales Manager Europe

ANSWER KEY

Practice 8

Stage 1: Identify the Task

Write an application letter. (In this case for a job as a secretary/receptionist).

Stage 2: Layout
- your address - 29 High Street, Ireland Wood, Leeds, LD9 2JP
- the date - 5th May 1988
- the name and address of the person to whom you are writing - Mrs Y Edwards, The National Trust Co, 2-10 Albert Street, Ashton, AS7 9EZ
- the correct salutation - Dear Mrs Edwards
- complimentary close - Yours sincerely
- a signature/name/position - (your signature and name)

Stage 3: Identify Relevant Information
- secretarial position
- aged 25
- good typing speeds
- word processing experience (Windows/Wordstar)
- shorthand
- fluent French and Russian
- Private Secretary's Certificate from LCCI
- 5 years as secretary to Marketing Manager at European Consultants
- most interested in using languages and computers
- responding to advert

Stage 4: Group/Order Relevant Information

1. Responding to advert.
2. Secretarial position.
3. 5 years experience as Marketing Manager's secretary.
4. Presently working for European Consultants.
5. Need change of position.
6. Private Secretary's Certificate from LCCI.
7. Word processing experience (Windows/Wordstar).
8. Shorthand.
9. Good typing speeds.
10. Fluent French and Russian.
11. Most interesting aspect would be using languages and expanding computing experience.

Stage 5:   Write the Letter

29 High Street
Ireland Wood
Leeds
LD9 2JP

5th May 1988

Mrs Y Edwards
The National Trust Co
2-10 Albert Street
Ashton
AS7 9EZ

Dear Mrs Edwards

I am writing to you in response to your advert for a secretary/receptionist which I saw in the Times today. I have been working as a secretary to the Marketing Manager at European Consultants for five years but am looking for a change in position so I can use my skills to their full potential.

I am a qualified secretary with the Private Secretary's Certificate from the London Chamber of Commerce and Industry. I have word processing experience with "Windows" and "Wordstar", shorthand and am a qualified typist. I can also speak fluent French and Russian.

The most interesting aspect of the work for me would be extending my computer experience and using my languages. I hope you will consider my application and I look forward to hearing from you.

Yours sincerely

(your signature)
(printed name)

ANSWER KEY

Practice 9

Stage 1: Identify the Task

Write a letter.

Stage 2: Layout

- your company address - Sheffield Bio-Technics Ltd, Moorside Industrial Estate, Sheffield, SD9 2PQ, England
- the date - 3rd May 1990
- the name and address of the person to whom you are writing - Mr R MacDonald - Managing Director, Woomera Bio-Technics Pty, 1 Rockingham Way, Melbourne, Victoria, Australia
- the correct salutation - Dear Mr MacDonald
- complimentary close - Yours sincerely
- signature/name/position - (your signature and name) Assistant Manager

Stage 3: Identify Relevant Information

- change of programme
- apologise for short notice
- changes to programme
  - Day 1 Camelot Hotel
  - Day 2 Leave hotel at 8.45.
          Meet Mr Brown, MD, and Mrs Sharp, General Manager
  - Day 3 Leave hotel at 8.45.
          Tour of factory and warehouse with Mr Smith, Production Manager
  - Day 4 Leave hotel at 8.45.
          Meeting at Head Office with Mr Taylor, Quality Manager and Mr Richards, Marketing Manager
  - Day 5 No changes

Stage 4: Group/Order Relevant Information

1. Change of programme.
2. Day 1 Camelot Hotel.
   Day 2 Leave hotel at 8.45. Meet Mr Brown, MD, and Mrs Sharp, General Manager.
   Day 3 Leave hotel at 8.45. Tour of factory and warehouse with Mr Smith, Production Manager.
   Day 4 Leave hotel at 8.45. Meeting at Head Office with Mr Taylor, Quality Manager and Mr Richards, Marketing Manager.
   Day 5 No changes.
3. Apologise for short notice and changes.

Section 1: Letters

Stage 5: Write the Letter

Sheffield Bio-Technics Ltd.
Moorside Industrial Estate
Sheffield
SD9 2PQ
England

3rd May 1990

Mr R MacDonald
Managing Director
Woomera Bio-Technics Pty
1 Rockingham Way
Melbourne
Victoria
Australia

Dear Mr MacDonald

I am writing to you to inform you of some changes to the programme. These changes are due to unforeseen circumstances and your new programme will be as follows:

Day 1   Flight arrival 1600. Our driver will meet you and take you to the **Camelot Hotel**.

Day 2   Leave hotel at **8.45**. Meeting at Head Office with **Mr Brown, Managing Director** and **Mrs Sharp, General Manager**.

Day 3   Leave hotel at **8.45**. Tour of factory and tour of warehouse with **Mr Smith, Production Manager**.

Day 4   Leave hotel at **8.45**. Meeting at Head Office with **Mr Taylor, Quality Manager** and **Mr Richards, Marketing Manager.**

Day 5   No changes.

I apologise for these changes at such short notice and hope they will not cause you any inconvenience.

Yours sincerely

(your signature)
(printed name)
Assistant Manager

ANSWER KEY

Practice 10

Stage 1: Identify the Task

Write the letter.

Stage 2: Layout

- your company address - International Assets, Trent Industrial Estate, Nottingham, NG7 2RA
- the date - 17th November 1989
- the name and address of the person to whom you are writing
- correct salutation - Dear Colleague
- complimentary close - Yours sincerely
- signature/name/position - leave space for signature, John Smith, Personnel Manager

Stage 3: Identify Relevant Information

- company's plans for factories
  - close factory in south
  - expand **one** in north
  - expand factory in west
- company's plans for workforce
  - no dismissals
  - relocation policy
  - early retirement policy
- figures 20,000 workers, 8,000 relocations, 4,000 retirements

Stage 4: Group/Order Relevant Information

1. Information of changes affecting colleagues.
2. Company's plans for factories:
   - close factory in south
   - expand factory in west
   - expand one in north/reduce the other in the north.
3. Company's plans for workforce:
   - no dismissals
   - relocation policy
   - early retirement policy.
4. Details: 20,000 workers, 8,000 relocations, 4,000 retirements.

Stage 5: Write the Letter

> International Assets
> Trent Industrial Estate
> Nottingham   NG7 2RA
>
> 17th November 1989
>
> Dear Colleague
>
> I am writing to inform you of some changes which, after much thought and consideration, will be introduced in order to secure our common future.
>
> First of all, it has been decided to close the factory in the south. However, the factory in the west will be expanding as will one of the factories in the north. The other factory in the north will be reduced by 2,000.
>
> It is company policy not to dismiss any staff in such situations, but rather to offer all staff the chance of early retirement or relocation. Of the 20,000 workers presently in employment it is planned that 8,000 will be relocated and 4,000 will be offered early retirement.
>
> I am sorry to inform you of these changes, however, they will secure the future of the company and our workers.
>
> Yours sincerely
>
>
> John Smith
> Personnel Manager

Section 2: Memos

ANSWER KEY

Section 2:   Memos

Practice 3

Stage 5:   Write the Memo

MEMO

To: All employees
From: (your name)
Subject: Smoking in offices
Date: (today's date)

Various objections to smoking in the offices, including it being unpleasant and dirty, were brought up at a recent staff/management meeting.

It was decided to find out everyone's opinion on this by sending out a questionnaire. You will find this on the tear-off slip below. A trial period will be based on the results and will last for three months. At the end of the trial period a final decision will be made on company policy regarding smoking in offices. Please return to Mr J Brown in Room 321 as soon as possible.

Name:

Please circle your choice: total ban on smoking / non-smoking areas / complete freedom

---

Practice 4

Stage 4:   Group/Order Relevant Information

1   Restaurant closed for one week, from next Monday.
2   Re-decoration.
3   Catering firm will provide drinks and sandwiches for morning and afternoon breaks.
4   Trolley near reception, first floor.
5   Lunches provided at Rafters Restaurant in the High Street.
6   Open 12pm - 1.00pm.
7   Special menu for employees.

Stage 5:   Write the Memo

MEMO

To: Peter MacParland, Office Manager
From: (your name), Catering Manager
Subject: Closure of staff restaurant
Date: (today's date)

The staff restaurant will be closed for one week from next Monday, for re-decoration. A catering firm will sell drinks and sandwiches from a trolley which will be located in the reception area on the first floor. They will be there during the morning and afternoon breaks.

Rafters Restaurant in the High Street will open their restaurant between 12 o'clock and 1 o'clock and will serve a special lunchtime menu for all employees at the usual prices.

ANSWER KEY

Practice 5

Stage 3: Identify Relevant Information

- monthly photocopying bill increased
- up from 10,000 to 18,000 copies per month
- more breakdowns of photocopier
- need to find out how many copies each member of staff makes
- need to get this under control
- Copyguard - small computer
- keeps records of how many copies each employee makes
- 6-figure access number for each employee
- typed into Copyguard to switch it on
- must have number to be able to use it
- from next Monday
- tear-off slip:
  - employee's name
  - job
  - 6-figure access number
- any questions contact me

Stage 4: Group/Order Relevant Information

1. Monthly photocopying bill increased.
2. Up from 10,000 to 18,000 per month.
3. More breakdowns.
4. Need to get system under control.
5. Need to find out how many copies each employee makes every week.
6. Introduce Copyguard.
7. Small computer.
8. Keeps record of how many copies each employee makes.
9. Employees need 6-figure access number.
10. Typed into Copyguard to access photocopier.
11. Must have number to be able to use it.
12. Tear-off slip:
    - name
    - job
    - 6-figure access number.
13. Any questions contact me.

Stage 5: Write the Memo

MEMO

To: All employees
From: (your name), Office Manager
Subject: Photocopying/Copyguard
Date:: (today's date)

Our monthly photocopying bill has increased tremendously over the past month. The number of copies has increased from 10,000 to 18,000 and this has led to many breakdowns.

To get this system under control and to find out how many photocopies each member of staff is making, we have decided to fit a "Copyguard" to the photocopier as of next Monday. This is a small computer which keeps a record of how many copies each employee makes. Every employee must have an individual 6-figure access number, which needs to be typed in to access the photocopier. Anyone without a number will not be able to use the photocopier.

On the tear-off slip at the bottom of this memo, write your name and job and the 6-figure number you have chosen. If you have any questions then contact my office.

Name ....

Job ....

Number .... / .... / .... / .... / ....

Section 2: Memos

Practice 6

Stage 2: Layout

To: Frank Chadburn, Managing Director
From: (your name), Office Manager
Subject: Recycling waste paper
Date: (today's date)

Stage 3: Identify Relevant Information

- introduce new scheme
- save waste paper for recycling
- value of waste paper
- environmental reasons
- saving trees
- containers on all floors
- emptied weekly
- can sell to recycling firm
- containers to be placed next to lifts

Stage 4: Group/Order Relevant Information

1. Introduce new scheme.
2. Save waste paper for recycling.
3. Environmental reasons.
4. Saving trees.
5. Value of waste paper.
6. Sell to recycling firms.
7. Containers on all floors.
8. Next to the lifts.
9. Emptied weekly.

Stage 5: Write the Memo

MEMO

To: Frank Chadburn, Managing Director
From: (your name), Office Manager
Subject: Recycling waste paper
Date: (today's date)

Last week's staff meeting decided to introduce a scheme to save waste paper for recycling, as a way of helping the environment.

There are many environmental reasons for this, not least, saving trees. The paper we save is also worth a lot to the company as we can sell it to a recycling firm who will place containers on all floors next to the lifts and will empty them once a week.

ANSWER KEY

Practice 7

Stage 1: Identify the Task

Write a memo.

Stage 2: Layout

To: Mr Ruru
From: (your name), Office Manager
Subject: Visit to Glenisla Electronics
Date: (today's date)

Stage 3: Identify Relevant information

- Glenisla Electronics
- supplies electrical systems to our company
- arranged 11.30am meeting, Mr Roberts, Development Manager
- leave Mr R's hotel 9.00am by car
- chauffeur to be back at 6.00pm
- unfortunately unable to dine with him tomorrow evening
- recommend Manuel's Restaurant or Taj Mahal
- both near main station
- 200m walking distance from hotel

Stage 4: Group/Order Relevant Information

1. Arranged 11.30am meeting with Mr Roberts, Development Manager.
2. Glenisla Electronics.
3. Supplies electrical systems to our company.
4. Chauffeur will collect you 9.00am at your hotel.
5. Expect to be back at 6.00pm.
6. Unfortunately unable to dine with you tomorrow evening.
7. Recommend Manuel's Restaurant or Taj Mahal.
8. Both near main station.
9. 200m walking distance from hotel.

Stage 5: Write the Memo

MEMO

To: Mr Ruru
From: (your name), Office Manager
Subject: Visit to Glenisla Electronics
Date: (today's date)

I have arranged a meeting at 11.30am tomorrow for you with Mr Roberts, Development Manager at Glenisla Electronics. They are our main supplier of electrical systems. Our chauffeur will collect you at your hotel at 9.00am and he will return you at about 6.00pm.

Unfortunately, I am unable to dine with you tomorrow evening, but I recommend Manuel's Restaurant for Spanish food or the Taj Mahal Restaurant if you like Indian food. Both are very near to the main station and within 200 metres of your hotel.

Section 2: Memos

Practice 8

Stage 1: Identify the Task

Write the memo.

Stage 2: Layout

To: All section leaders
From: (your name), Manager
Subject: Punctuality
Date: (today's date)

Stage 3: Identify Relevant Information

- members of staff arriving late
- offices not opening on time
- customers having to wait
- members of staff who are on time unhappy
- customer complaints
- action needs to be taken

Stage 4: Group/Order Relevant Information

1. Offices not opening on time.
2. Members of staff arriving late.
3. Members of staff who are on time unhappy.
4. Customer complaints.
5. Customers having to wait.
6. Action needs to be taken.

Stage 5: Write the Memo

MEMO

To: All section leaders
From: (your name), Manager
Subject: Punctuality
Date: (today's date)

It has come to my attention that some offices are not opening on time because many members of staff are arriving late. This not only means that members of staff who are on time have more work to do but we have also had many complaints from customers that they have had to wait to speak to someone.

This situation is not acceptable and you must take some action to improve staff punctuality.

ANSWER KEY

Practice 9

Stage 1: Identify the Task

Write a memo.

Stage 2: Layout

To: All staff
From: (your name), Office Manager
Subject: Vending machines
Date: (today's date)

Stage 3: Identify Relevant Information

- introduce vending machines
- two on each floor
- possible to get drinks at any time
- also biscuits/crisps/chocolate, etc
- new, better system
- old system to be changed
- hot drinks often cold
- tea ladies will not lose jobs
- work in canteen preparing lunches

Stage 4: Group/Order Relevant Information

1. Old system to be changed.
2. Hot drinks often cold.
3. New, better system.
4. Introduce vending machines.
5. Two on each floor.
6. Possible to get drinks at any time.
7. Also soft drinks.
8. Also biscuits/crisps/chocolate.
9. Tea ladies will not lose jobs.
10. Work in canteen preparing lunch.

Stage 5: Write the Memo

MEMO

To: All staff
From: (your name), Office Manager
Subject: Vending machines
Date: (today's date)

It has been decided to change the old system of providing hot drinks and snacks. The hot drinks from the trolleys were often cold because the tea ladies had to push their trolleys around the building.

The new, better system will see the introduction of vending machines, two on each floor, so that you can get drinks at any time. Tea and coffee, as well as soft drinks, biscuits, crisps and chocolate, will be available from the machines.

This does not mean that the tea ladies will lose their jobs as they can now work in the canteen preparing lunch.

Section 2: Memos

Practice 10

Stage 1: Identify the Task

Write a memo.

Stage 2: Layout

To: Ralph Charrer, Chief Caretaker
From: (your name), Office Manager
Subject: Chairman's visit
Date: (today's date)

Stage 3: Identify Relevant Information

- Chairman's visit next week
- last visit
- keen on appearances
- spotlessly clean
- building must be in perfect order
- especially main reception area
- corridors and lifts too
- staff restaurant where he will have lunch also important

Stage 4: Group/Order Relevant Information

1. Chairman's visit next week.
2. Last visit.
3. Keen on appearances.
4. Spotlessly clean.
5. Building must be in perfect order.
6. Especially main reception area.
7. Corridors and lifts too.
8. Staff restaurant where he will have lunch also important.

Stage 5: Write the Memo

MEMO

To: Ralph Charrer, Chief Caretaker
From: (your name), Office Manager
Subject: Chairman's visit
Date: (today's date)

Next week our Chairman will visit our company and you remember how particular he was on his last visit. He's very keen on appearances and everything must be spotlessly clean. The whole building must be in perfect order.

Pay special attention to the main reception area, all corridors and lifts and in particular the staff restaurant where he will have lunch.

ANSWER KEY

ANSWER KEY

Practice 3

Stage 3: Write the Answers

Section 3: Short Answers

1	£1.85.
2	The Post Office.
3	Free of charge.
4	Phone 0800 581960.
5	a Yes.
	b They receive special treatment.
6	They are immediately transferred and separately processed.
7	DL (10cm x 21.5cm)/C5 (16.5 cm x 23cm)/C4 (23cm x 33cm).
8	If the value is over £270.
9	Red SwiftAir express label/Blue Airmail label.
10	Add stamps to the value of the extra postage.
11	SWIFTPACKS, FREEPOST, The Publicity Centre, Fenton Way, Basildon, ESSEX, SS15 4BR.
12	Write to the address above/Ring 0800 581960.
13	It is a priority letter service.

Practice 4

Stage 2: Before you Start

Have you read through **all** the questions?
Have you read through **all** the information?

Stage 3: Write the Answers

1	Yes.
2	Yes.
3	Yes.
4	Yes.
5	Yes.
6	Switzerland/Germany.
7	Lower.
8	Portugal/Italy/Spain.
9	Contact the Ministry of Foreign Affairs or Danish Embassy or Consulate General.
10	2.5% - 3%.
11	None.
12	No.
13	2000.
14	No.
15	340 million.

Section 3: Short Answers

Practice 5

Stage 1: Identify the Task
Answer the questions briefly but precisely.

Stage 2: Before you Start
Have you read through **all** the questions?
Have you read through **all** the information?

Stage 3: Write the Answers

1	Week 1, Saturday, 09.00-12.30.
2	Week 2, Friday, 18.00.
3	Yes, Week 2, Friday, 17.00-18.00.
4	Week 1, Wednesday, 13.45-15.45.
5	Yes, 15.45-16.00.
6	Week 1, Wednesday, 08.30-10.00.
7	2 single sessions.
8	Week 1, Friday, 08.30-10.00.
9	3 hours in total. Week 2, Friday, 13.45-17.00.
10	Week 1, Monday, 11.15-12.45.

Practice 6

Stage 1: Identify the Task
Answer the questions briefly but precisely.

Stage 2: Before you Start
Have you read through **all** the questions?
Have you read through **all** the information?

Stage 3: Write the Answers

1	3.
2	International Cashless Calling.
3	Over 180.
4	International Direct Dialling.
5	No.
6	Most British Telecom Phones.
7	At least £1.00.
8	The UK international operator.
9	An operator in your own country.
10	Call Collect/Charge to your telephone credit card.
11	Your country code/Your area code/Your local number.
12	No.
13	No.
14	No cash required.
15	Home Direct Operator. Because you can speak to the operator in your own language.

ANSWER KEY

Practice 7

Stage 1: Identify the Task
Answer the questions briefly but precisely.

Stage 2: Before you Start
Have you read through **all** the questions?
Have you read through **all** the information?

Stage 3: Write the Answers

1	Yes.
2	EC$50.
3	BWIA/Aeropostal.
4	440 2796/7.
5	No restriction.
6	No.
7	Yes.
8	No.
9	Point Salines International Airport/South-west tip of Grenada.
10	In most.
11	The International Airport in Barbados.
12	All banks are open until 12.00. Some are open until 2.00.
13	EC$25.00.
14	No.
15	EC$ 1 is US$ .37.

Practice 8

Stage 1: Identify the Task
Answer the questions briefly but precisely.

Stage 2: Before you Start
Have you read through **all** the questions?
Have you read through **all** the information?

Stage 3: Write the Answers

1	Yes.	11	15.
2	0.	12	0.
3	February.	13	0.
4	Technical.	14	2.
5	19.	15	1.
6	2.	16	16.
7	2.	17	Yes.
8	28th February.	18	Yes.
9	Yes.	19	Yes.
10	It was a Public Holiday.	20	13th May.

Section 3: Short Answers

Practice 9

Stage 1: Identify the Task

Answer the questions briefly but precisely.

Stage 2: Before you Start

Have you read through **all** the questions?
Have you read through **all** the information?

Stage 3: Write the Answers

1	Section 3	Sub Section 8.2
2	Section 3	Sub Section 7.3
3	Section 2	Sub Section 6.15
4	Section 2	Sub Section 3.1
5	Section 3	SubSection 3.10/3.12
6	Section 1	Sub Section 2.5
7	Section 3	Sub Section 1
8	Section 2	Sub Section 2.1
9	Section 1	Sub Section 2.5
10	Section 2	Sub Section 6.18
11	Section 2	Sub Section 1.4
12	Section 1	Sub Section 1.9
13	Section 1	Sub Section 3
14	Section 2	Sub Section 2.8
15	Section 3	Sub Section 19.2
16	Section 3	Sub Section 3.1
17	Section 2	Sub Section 2.4
18	Section 1	Sub Section 2.5
19	Section 3	Sub Section 14.3
20	Section 3	Sub Section 11.3

Practice 10

Stage 1: Identify the Task

Answer the questions briefly but precisely.

Stage 2: Before you Start

Have you read through **all** the questions?
Have you read through **all** the information?

Stage 3: Write the Answers

1	There is a slight antipathy.
2	No.
3	Bottle of whisky for the host/ Chocolates for the hostess.
4	Because they are conscious of their geographical isolation.
5	New Zealanders.
6	Several hours.
7	High.
8	Most.
9	The host.
10	Yes.
11	Most.
12	No.
13	No.
14	Canberra.
15	Six states/Two territories.

ANSWER KEY

ANSWER KEY   Section 4:   True or False

Practice 3

Stage 3: Write the Answers

1	False	The extract is from a tapescript.
2	False	Andy Kenyon and Dr Richardson are Dr Standen's clinical research assistants.
3	False	Peter Coldwell does Phase 3 only.
4	False	Paul Booth is Peter Coldwell's assistant.
5	True	He joined us from Glucon Plc.
6	False	Peter Coldwell works for Germany.
7	False	Lisab is our new painkiller.
8	True	Jim Flavell is Medical Advisor.
9	False	Dr Horton is Medical Director.
10	False	Paul Booth works for ICI.

Practice 4

Stage 2: Before you Start

Have you read through **all** the statements?
Have you read through **all** the information?

Stage 3: Write the Answers

1	True	6000 people working in harbours and on ferries will lose their jobs.
2	True	Some Britons might commute from northern France.
3	False	Folkestone with Beussingue Portal near Calais.
4	False	Margaret Thatcher was the Prime Minister.
5	False	It is for maintenance and emergency access.
6	False	6500 British and 3500 French workers.
7	False	Not June 1993 as planned but winter 1993.
8	False	London will gain more.
9	False	A boom in the property market is expected.
10	True	Estimated at £20 billion it could reach £35 billion.

Section 4: True or False

Practice 5

Stage 1: Identify the Task
Say whether the statements are true or false.

Stage 2: Before you Start
Have you read through **all** the statements?
Have you read through **all** the information?

Stage 3: Write the Answers

A			B			C			
	1	a half		6	more		16	True	From 48% to 34%
	2	a third		7	the same		17	True	From 63% to 43%
	3	two thirds		8	more		18	False	It remained the same - 32%
	4	one third		9	less		19	False	It increased from 25% to 40%
	5	a half		10	more		20	True	30% in 1968 to 25% in 1988
		a third		11	the same				
				12	the same				
				13	less				
				14	more				
				15	more				

Practice 6

Stage 1: Identify the Task
Say whether the statements are true or false.

Stage 2: Before you Start
Have you read through **all** the statements?
Have you read through **all** the information?

Stage 3: Write the Answers

1	**False**	Buyz and Ecognom have done so since 1988.
2	**False**	More than 10% of its customers use them.
3	**False**	Credit cards are popular with people who buy in bulk.
4	**False**	Customers are using the cards more responsibly.
5	**False**	Next month.
6	**False**	They accept them in twelve outlets.
7	**False**	They have negotiated a reduction in the fee they have to pay.
8	**False**	Tristans have lagged behind their rivals.
9	**True**	They had good experience with direct debit cards.
10	**True**	They think it will bring in new customers.

ANSWER KEY

Practice 7

Stage 1: Identify the Task

Say whether the statements are true or false.

Stage 2: Before you Start

Have you read through **all** the statements?
Have you read through **all** the information?

Stage 3: Write the Answers

1	False	Only the manager or his/her deputy can.
2	False	One fire alarm call point should be tested weekly.
3	True	They must know how to use fire extinguishers.
4	False	They must not be used as door stops.
5	True	Only members of the fire-fighting party.
6	False	They both have to be checked weekly.
7	True	Every six months at the same time as the fire drill.
8	False	It must be kept in the manager's office ready for inspection by the Fire Brigade.
9	False	They must never be less than 1 metre.
10	True	Highly inflammable material must be kept away from fluorescent lights.

Practice 8

Stage 1: Identify the Task

Say whether the statements are true or false.

Stage 2: Before you Start

Have you read through **all** the statements?
Have you read through **all** the information?

Stage 3: Write the Answers

1	True	From the start it proved popular.
2	False	They are also announced on a public address system.
3	False	Train Captains check tickets and answer queries.
4	True	All stations have special lifts.
5	False	Alarm buttons are provided on trains and stations.
6	False	It is also carried out after 9.30pm.
7	False	Coin-operated ticket machines are provided in station entrance halls.
8	False	They may have to pay 10 times the value of the fare avoided.
9	False	They are also valid on British Railways.
10	False	They can be bought on the day from the DLR Information Centres.

Section 4: True or False

Practice 9

Stage 2: Before you Start

Have you read through **all** the statements?
Have you read through **all** the information?

Stage 3: Write the Answers

1	**True**	All you need to do is complete the request form overleaf.
2	**True**	You can call the UK from 120 countries overseas.
3	**False**	With a BT Chargecard you can also use fax machines.
4	**True**	You make quick calls to a number of your choice without having to dial the whole number.
5	**False**	The maximum daily allowance is £99.
6	**False**	There are over 30 million phones in the UK.
7	**False**	Dialling with a BT Chargecard costs the same as calling from a BT public payphone.
8	**False**	You can reclaim VAT on calls made via public payphones.
9	**False**	You can request any number of cards and it won't cost you anything.
10	**False**	You get an itemised statement of your calls.

Practice 10

Stage 1: Identify the Task

Say whether the statements are true or false.

Stage 2: Before you Start

Have you read through all the statements?
Have you read through all the information?

Stage 3: Write the Answers

1	**False**	The extract mentions account executives and upwards.
2	**False**	An unofficial flexitime system operates.
3	**True**	Big accounts include Lloyds Bank.
4	**False**	Subsidised canteen.
5	**False**	Staff squash club on premises.
6	**False**	Minimum of £10,000.
7	**False**	4 weeks compared to 35 days.
8	**True**	£2.3 million compared to £2.1 million.
9	**False**	Account executives and upwards have cars.
10	**True**	55% men, 45% women.

ANSWER KEY

ANSWER KEY

Section 5: Gap-Fills

Practice 3

Stage 3: Write the Answers

1	main	11	mezzanine
2	ground	12	Squirrel Computers
3	13	13	4
4	A	14	Desk Top Publishing
5	F	15	28
6	stands	16	5
7	general	17	18
8	right	18	7
9	A3	19	far
10	6	20	station

Practice 4

Stage 2: Before you Start

Have you read through **all** the information?
Have you looked at the table?

Stage 3: Write the Answers

1	same	11	lowest
2	all	12	half
3	except	13	amount
4	different	14	£9600
5	highest	15	£6483
6	lowest	16	1/3
7	£700	17	same
8	No	18	ago
9	two	19	much
10	July	20	whole

Practice 5

Stage 1: Identify the Task

Write the answer for each numbered space.

Stage 2: Before you Start

Have you read through **all** the information?
Have you looked at the table?

Stage 3: Write the Answers

1	half	11	left
2	broken	12	more
3	use	13	personal
4	shop	14	service
5	service	15	price
6	top	16	however
7	speed	17	less
8	at tills	18	lay out
9	however	19	quickly
10	more	20	equally

Practice 6

Stage 1: Identify the Task

Write the answer for each numbered space.

Stage 2: Before you Start

Have you read through **all** the information?
Have you looked at the bar chart?

Stage 3: Write the Answers

1	total	11	higher
2	more	12	followed
3	highest	13	FR Germany
4	equal	14	least
5	five	15	low
6	lowest	16	76
7	twice	17	USSR
8	highest	18	just
9	according	19	average
10	many	20	all

Section 5: Gap Fills

Practice 7

Stage 1: Identify the Task
Write the answer for each numbered space.

Stage 2: Before you Start
Have you read through **all** the information?
Have you looked at the table?

Stage 3: Write the Answers

1	14.5	11	Western Europe
2	3.0 million	12	over three
3	4	13	Western Europe
4	than	14	than
5	leisure	15	rose
6	from	16	doubled
7	300	17	more
8	twice	18	preceding
9	five	19	decrease
10	six	20	1984

Practice 8

Stage 1: Identify the Task
Write the answer for each numbered space.

Stage 2: Before you Start
Have you read through **all** the information?
Have you looked at the timetable?

Stage 3: Write the Answers

1	BUE	11	daily non-stop
2	0910 Mon/Wed/Fri	12	winter
3	Lagos	13	3
4	13.45	14	week
5	Thursdays	15	11.15
6	4	16	Gatwick
7	Harare	17	2
8	more	18	Heathrow
9	12.40	19	2
10	Tuesdays	20	October 1991

Practice 9

Stage 1: Identify the Task
Write the answer for each numbered space.

Stage 2: Before you Start
Have you read through **all** the information?
Have you looked at the table?

Stage 3: Write the Answers

A		**B**	
1	more	6	camcorder
2	less	7	highest
3	less	8	three
4	more	9	£19.95
5	more	10	£17.95

C		**D**	
11	higher	16	higher
12	higher	17	lower
13	lower	18	lower
14	lower	19	lower
15	higher	20	lower

Practice 10

Stage 1: Identify the Task
Write the answer for each numbered space.

Stage 2: Before you Start
Have you read through **all** the information?
Have you looked at the diagram?

Stage 3: Write the Answers

1	a	£1.98	7	l	VAT
	b	£2.02		m	duty
				n	£1.07
2	c	less			
3	d	75	8	o	202
	e	10			
	f	3			
			9	p	the government
4	g	88 pence		q	petrol stations
				r	oil companies
5	h	7			
6	i	over	10	s	the government
	j	duty		t	the oil companies
	k	value added			

ANSWER KEY

ANSWER KEY

Practice 3

Stage 3: Write the Answers

1	Gerry Hitchens
2	Heathrow Airport
3	June 5th
4	Anne Drews
5	Lancaster Computers
6	Aston Tower, 145 MacParland Avenue, Manchester MVR 14U
7	Purchasing Department
8	Chief Buyer
9	AD 40/the Empress/Ultra Clean Emsworth
10	Yes
11	Yes
12	Yes
13	No
14	No

Section 6: Forms and Diagrams

Practice 4

Stage 2: Before you Start

Have you read through **all** the information?
Have you looked at the form?

Stage 3: Write the Answers

1	PETER KIRK
2	BARBICAN INTEROP TRADE FAIR
3	15 JAN
4	DR JAMES PICKERING
5	ARKON US
6	C/O COMMERCIAL ATTACHE US EMBASSY, GROSVENOR SQUARE, LONDON, W1
7	MARKETING DEPARTMENT
8	ACCOUNT EXECUTIVE
9	INTERCOM SYSTEMS/ALARMS AND MASTER CLOCKS
10	YES
11	YES
12	YES
13	NO
14	NO

Section 6: Forms and Diagrams

Practice 5

Stage 1: Identify the Task
Complete the form.

Stage 2: Before you Start
Have you read through **all** the information?
Have you looked at the form?

Stage 3: Write the Answers

ORDER FORM			
Item Code	Description	Quantity	Price (£)
1 F1234	3-Drawer Filing Cabinet - grey/green	4	339
2 F1111	Typist Chairs (Red)	20	1100
3 F1627	M1 Fax	1	575
4 S6198	Fax Rolls	20	120
5 F1588	Calculators	60	600
6 S5467	Binder	2	398
7 G36871	Overhead Projector	1	249
8 F1360	Shredder	2	240
9 J1234	Wall Clock (Pine)	2	50
10 S5674	Flipchart	3	180
		Sub Total	**3851**
		Less Discount	**385**
		Delivery Charge	**NIL**
		TOTAL	**3466**

Practice 6

Stage 1: Identify the Task
Complete the form.

Stage 2: Before you Start
Have you read through **all** the information?
Have you looked at the form?

Stage 3: Write the Answers

1	EXECUTIVE SECRETARY PROGRAMME	8	CARSTEN BROS
2	THE METROPOLE, BRIGHTON	9	LAKE VIEW TOWER, MEADOWCOURT AVENUE, LONDON, SE3 9EU
3	MS	10	081 318 5633
4	HEYWORTH	11	COFFEE AND TEA IMPORTERS
5	JANE	12	JAMES KIRK, PERSONNEL MANAGER
6	PA	13	YES
7	SALES DEPARTMENT	14	ON ACCOUNT

183

ANSWER KEY

Practice 7

Stage 1: Identify the Task
Complete the diagram.

Stage 2: Before you Start
Have you read through **all** the information?
Have you looked at the diagram?

Stage 3: Write the Answers

1	PA
2	Melissa Andrews
3	Jack Hughes
4	Administration Manager
5	Richard Blane
6	Brendan Charles
7	Mike Foster
8	John Kane
9	Ralph Charrer
10	Paula Essex
11	Vic Crowe
12	Jim Dugdale
13	Alan Deakin
14	Institute Director
15	Dr Martin
16	Foundation Council
17	Part-time
18	Europe
19	Amsterdam
20	Security Chief

Practice 8

Stage 1: Identify the Task
Put the letter next to each number.

Stage 2: Before you Start
Have you read through **all** the information?
Have you looked at the diagram?

Stage 3: Write the Answers

1	G
2	Q
3	O
4	N
5	E
6	S
7	I
8	T
9	D
10	C
11	H
12	F
13	R
14	A
15	M
16	L
17	P
18	J
19	K
20	B

Section 6: Forms and Diagrams

Practice 9

Stage 1: Identify the Task
Complete your pocket diary.

Stage 2: Before you Start
Have you read through **all** the information?
Have you looked at the plan?

Stage 3: Write the Answers

1	Cancel Staff Meeting on 10th
2	Lunch with Peter 12.30pm
3	2.30pm Finance Committee Meeting
4	10 am - 4 pm Staff Inductions (3 people)
5	10 am - 4 pm Staff Inductions (3 people)
6	10.00am Staff Appraisals
7	Free
8	2.30pm Finance Committee Meeting
9	Get Carol to check Andy's service
10	Andy leaving
11	Free
12	Free
13	2.30pm Finance Committee Meeting
14	Fax Kirk's article to Glasgow
15	Kirk's article due in Glasgow
16	10.00 am Staff Appraisals
17	Day off
18	2.30pm Finance Committee Meeting
19	Auditors in Company
20	Auditors in Company

Practice 10

Stage 1: Identify the Task
Complete the form.

Stage 2: Before you Start
Have you read through **all** the information?
Have you looked at the form?

Stage 3: Write the Answers

1	2 - 5
2	Yes
3	1 IBM and 1 Squirrel
4	MD/Warehousing/Stock Control
5	Stock Control Better Presentation Design
6	1 - 5
7	51+
8	£2,001+
9	JAMES T KIRK
10	MANAGING DIRECTOR
11	KIRK AND STEVENS
12	51 MARISCHAL ROAD, LONDON
13	SE19 7KS
14	081 318 5634
15	BREWING

ANSWER KEY

SERIES 4 EXAMINATION 1993

Friday 12 November

**FIRST LEVEL
ENGLISH FOR BUSINESS**

(Code No: 1041)

Question Number	Examiners Use Only
1	
2	
3	
4	
TOTAL	

Instructions to Candidates

(a) The time allowed for this examination is 2 hours.

(b) Answer all **4** questions.

(c) Use the spaces provided in the combined question and answer booklet to complete the questions. If more space is needed for answers or rough notes, use the supplementary sheets provided and secure them inside your booklet with your name and candidate number clearly written on each sheet. Rough notes should be clearly crossed through.

(d) Credit will be given for correct spelling, punctuation and grammar.

(e) Adequate and appropriate communication is required rather than a particular number of words.

(f) When you finish, check your work carefully.

ENTER DETAILS BELOW

CANDIDATE'S NAME IN FULL
as it is to appear on the certificate   Identity Card Number..................................

Subject Code Number ......**1041**...

Candidate's Number ....   Centre Code ....

Full Private Address ....
....   Post Code ....

Centre Name and Address ....
....

State here the number of additional sheets handed in. ☐

1041/4/93   1   OVER

QUESTION 1

Situation You are Director of Personnel in a large insurance company. Internal reports and customer quotations are typed centrally in a typing section led by Joan Wolding. Recently some department managers have complained to you about the quality of the typing, the late return of the work and the rude attitude of Miss Wolding when asked for help.

Task Write a **memo** to Joan Wolding detailing some of the complaints referred to above and reminding her that she should be more helpful to managers who come to her. Make up any necessary details.

Use the space below to write your memo.

MEMORANDUM

1041/4/93   2   **CONTINUED ON NEXT PAGE**

QUESTION 1 Continued

You may use this page to continue the memo if necessary.

(30 marks)

QUESTION 2

Situation You are checking the information in a brochure for UK based members of Club Ulisse, which is organised by Alitalia.

Task Use the information opposite to say whether the following statements are **true** or **false**. Put **true** or **false** and give **brief** details to justify your answer in the spaces provided.

1	0800 353535 is the telephone number of Alitalia in Italy.
2	The Club Ulisse hotline telephone number is a Rome number.
3	The Club Ulisse hotline is open 24 hours a day during the week.
4	The UK Alitalia ticket office is at Gatwick Airport.
5	Tickets bought by credit card can be sent by post.
6	The maximum discount available for Club Ulisse members staying at Sheraton hotels is 50%.
7	To get a Sheraton discount you must send your Club Ulisse card to the hotel when booking.
8	Even if you have a Sheraton International Club card you still have to pay for your newspaper when staying in the Sheraton hotels.
9	With a Club Ulisse card you can check out of a Sheraton hotel as late as 4pm on your first visit.
10	The points you can get with a Sheraton International Club card can be used to buy presents from the Sheraton Club catalogue.

(30 marks)

QUESTION 2   Continued

When you need a ticket in a hurry

Sometimes, urgent meetings demand that your flight arrangements have to be made at the very last minute. In such cases if you are unable to get your ticket through your usual travel agent, Club Ulisse can solve the problem by giving you the facility to purchase your ticket over the telephone, utilising your dedicated Club hotline number in the UK 071-602-9396. Then collect your ticket at the Alitalia Heathrow office, next to the check-in desks at Terminal 2.

All you need to do is quote your credit card number over the telephone, then present the card when collecting your ticket.

If you have the luxury of a little more time, you can still use your credit card to purchase tickets over the phone and we can then post them direct to your home or office.

The Club Ulisse hotline is open from 8.30am to 6.30pm on weekdays and from 9.00am to 2.00pm on Saturdays. If you need to book a ticket outside of these times you may call the Alitalia Ticket Office at Heathrow Airport on 081 745 8469/497.

Hotel Discounts

We have negotiated a great deal for Club Ulisse members staying at Sheraton Hotels worldwide.

Now, whenever you stay at one of the Sheraton properties you will be able to claim a discount of between 20% and 45%.

Furthermore, after your first stay at any of the listed Sheraton Hotels you will automatically receive the Sheraton International Club card. This will entitle you to:

- upgrading whenever possible
- a check-out time extended to 1600 hours
- free newspaper daily
- 4 points for every $ spent on services during the stay

The points can be converted into vouchers for future stays at Sheraton Hotels, or can be used to purchase gifts from the Sheraton Club catalogue.

You may book your hotel room through Alitalia at the same time as your flight, or through Sheraton on their centralised reservations line 0800 353535. In order to receive the discount simply quote your membership number when booking and show your Club Ulisse card when checking in.

QUESTION 3

Situation As Training Officer for your company you receive details of courses and seminars in 1994.

Task Look at the list of courses and seminars opposite and answer the questions below **in the spaces provided**.

	QUESTIONS	ANSWERS
1	Who will organise the seminar on '1994 and Beyond'?	
2	How many training sessions will the CIMA organise?	
3	How many training sessions will be held in Oxford?	
4	Who will organise the seminar on Retail Marketing?	
5	How many seminars will be held in August?	
6	Where can I hear about the Social Charter?	
7	Is the Warwick Business School organising any seminars?	
8	Is there a seminar on 'Financial Reporting in Belgium'?	
9	What is the phone number for the CIMA?	
10	Will there be a seminar on Visual Display Screens in the South East?	
11	Will there be a seminar on EMC Awareness in the West Midlands?	
12	Who will organise the Environmental audit session?	
13	Will the Retail Marketing session be held in June or July?	
14	Where can I hear about Euromec 94?	
15	What seminar are Allington Events Ltd organising?	
16	How can I contact ROSPA?	
17	Will ROSPA organise any events in London?	
18	Is there a seminar on Export Finance in Oxford?	
19	What is the subject of the last seminar in July?	
20	Which number do I ring for information on the seminar on June 16?	

(20 marks)

QUESTION 3 CONTINUED

DATE	VENUE	ORGANISING BODY	TOPIC	CONTACT TEL NO
South East				
4 June	London	Chartered Institute of Management Accountants (CIMA)	Financial reporting in France	071 637 2311
4 June	London	Solicitors European Group	UK sovereignty	0483 57611
5 June	London	Chartered Institute of Management Accountants	Financial reporting in Spain	071 637 2311
10 June	London	Chartered Institute of Management Accountants	Financial reporting in Germany	071 637 2311
10 June	London	BEAMA	Public procurement	071 872 6264
12 June	Oxford	Oxford and Buckinghamshire 1994 Club	Environmental audit	0865 244977
12 June	London	London Business School	Economic information	071 262 5050
16 June	London	London Chamber of Commerce	Export finance	071 248 4444 ext 2093
18 June	London	Solicitors European Group	1994 and Beyond	0483 57611
22 June	Watford	Institute of Grocery Distribution	Retail marketing	0923 857141
22 June	London	Chartered Institute of Management Accountants	Corporation tax	071 637 2311
23 June	London	Local Economy Policy Unit	Labour markets	071 928 8989 ext 2736
23 June	London	Chartered Institute of Management Accountants	VAT	071 637 2311
24 June	Guilford	Impact Europe	Social Charter	081 394 3267
29 June	Southampton	Allington Events Ltd	Euromec 94	0703 771560
30 June	London	Institute of Electrical Engineers	EMC awareness	0438 313311
6 July	London	Solicitors European Group	EC competition law	0483 57611
6 July	London	Institute of Personnel Management	EC recruitment	081 946 9100
6 July	Oxford	ADA Management	Education and training	0495 753716
8 July	London	BEAMA	Mutual Acceptance of Electrotechnical Products	071 872 6239
10 August	London	Institute of Personnel Management	Managing Employees in Europe	081 946 9100
West Midlands				
17 June	Birmingham	ROSPA	Visual display screens	021 200 2461
17 June	Birmingham	ROSPA	Manual handling of loads	021 200 2461
18 June	Warwick	ADA Management	Education and training	0494 753716

1041/4/93

OVER

QUESTION 4

Situation: You work in the Public Relations Department of Kirk & Sons and are at the moment arranging a marketing conference. Over the weekend you make notes about the various speakers.

Task: Use the notes below to complete the conference timetable opposite in **block capitals**. The usual format is to state the title of the session, followed by the person responsible and finally the type of session (lecture etc.)

Write your answers in the spaces provided.

And then, after the Plenary Session, we'll split up. The 3 lectures will all be in the larger room, which means that the two workshops before lunch and the case study after will be in the other. Then, finally, Sir John's brother, James, will give the closing remarks.

Now, Stanley Accrington wants the first lecture. That's on the "Marketing Mix", and Paul Paynter wants the 11.10 slot for his workshop on "Client Care". So I'll put Alexander Crewe to follow Accringtonn. His title is "Product Life Cycle".

Which means that the first workshop will be Percy Grundy's on "New Product Launch".

I can save the best lecture till after lunch: Bill Martin on "International Marketing". So Lester Blakeney has the alternative. He hasn't decided which of his 'portfolio' he's going to do, so I'll have to announce that later.

(20 marks)

QUESTION 4 CONTINUED

PLENARY SESSION

9.00	Welcome
	Sir John Kirk

	DUGDALE ROOM (150 seats)	**DEAKIN ROOM** (45 seats)
9.15	....	....
to	by	by ....
11.00	....	....
11.10	....	....
to	by	by ....
12.00	....	....

LUNCH

2.00	....	....
to	by	by ....
4.00	....	....

CLOSING REMARKS

4.15 ....

Other titles available from Logophon.

Business Introduction
ISBN 3-922514-18-9

Targeting Britain
ISBN 3-922514-19-7

How to Pass - Spoken English for Industry and Commerce
Preliminary Level, Student's Book, ISBN 3-922514-33-2

How to Pass - Spoken English for Industry and Commerce
Preliminary Level, Teachers Book, ISBN 3-922514-37-5

How to Pass - Spoken English for Industry and Commerce
Preliminary Level, Student's Cassette, ISBN 3-922514-38-3

How to Pass - Spoken English for Industry and Commerce
Preliminary Level, Pictures Book, ISBN 3-922514-39-1

How to Pass - Spoken English for Industry and Commerce
Threshold Level, Student's Book, ISBN 3-922514-34-0

How to Pass - Spoken English for Industry and Commerce
Threshold Level, Teachers Book, ISBN 3-922514-40-5

How to Pass - Spoken English for Industry and Commerce
Threshold Level, Student's Cassette, ISBN 3-922514-41-3

How to Pass - Spoken English for Industry and Commerce
Threshold Level, Picture Book, ISBN 3-922514-42-1

How to Pass - Spoken English for Industry and Commerce
Intermediate Level, Student's Book, ISBN 3-922514-35-9

How to Pass - Spoken English for Industry and Commerce
Intermediate Level, Teachers Book, ISBN 3-922514-43-x

How to Pass - Spoken English for Industry and Commerce
Intermediate Level, Student's Cassette, ISBN 3-922514-44-8

How to Pass - Spoken English for Industry and Commerce
Advanced Level, Student's Book, ISBN 3-922514-36-7

How to Pass - Spoken English for Industry and Commerce
Advanced Level, Teachers Book, ISBN 3-922514-45-6

How to Pass - Spoken English for Industry and Commerce
Advanced Level, Student's Cassette, ISBN 3-922514-46-4

Logophon Lehrmittel Verlag GmbH
Alte Gärtnerei 2

55118 Mainz, Germany

Tel: +49-6131-71645
Fax: +49-6131-72596